INSPIRATION CONTAGION

HEALTH SECRETS
FOR RAVING SUCCESS

HOLLY JEAN JACKSON

INSPIRATION CONTAGION

HEALTH SECRETS
FOR RAVING SUCCESS

HOLLY JEAN JACKSON

Inspiration Contagion

Health Secrets for Raving Success

Holly Jean Jackson

©Copyright 2022 Holly Jean Jackson

Published by Brave Healer Productions

Paperback ISBN: 978-1-954047-44-0

eBook ISBN: 978-1-954047-45-7

TABLE OF CONTENTS

DISCLAIMER

This book offers health and nutritional information and is designed for educational purposes only. You should not rely on this information as a substitute for, nor does it replace professional medical advice, diagnosis, or treatment. If you have any concerns or questions about your health, you should always consult with a physician or other healthcare professional. Do not disregard, avoid, or delay obtaining medical or health-related advice from your healthcare professional because of something you may have read here. The use of any information provided in this book is solely at your own risk.

Developments in medical research may impact the health, fitness, and nutritional advice that appears here. No assurances can be given that the information contained in this book will always include the most relevant findings or developments with respect to the particular material.

Having said all that, know that I have shared my tools, practices, and knowledge with you with a sincere and generous intent to assist you on your health and wellness journey. Please contact me with any questions you may have about the techniques or information provided. I will be happy to assist you further!

PREFACE

THE IMPORTANCE OF THE CAMPFIRE,
STORYTELLING, AND COMMUNITY

*"The work of the individual still remains the spark
that moves mankind forward.*

~ IGOR SIKORSKY

For many years I've had countless friends, acquaintances, colleagues, and strangers tell me, "Holly, you need to write a book." It comes up in conversation after I share a story. Usually, it's the bear story and sometimes a story about dealing with chronic pain.

Every time I would attempt to write this book, I was writing from the perspective of invisible and chronic pain. I would get going and then quickly discover that writing about my pain and suffering from the past was depleting and exhausting. It wasn't life-giving. It was painful.

Now that I am a bit wiser, I chose to start from my meditation cushion. I began visualizing what I wanted to share. The essence I wanted people to walk away with. The feelings I wanted to stir up inside of others.

I realized quickly that what I really wanted to write about was *inspiration*—how people can go through wild, crazy, and painful experiences and instill inspiration, encouragement, and wisdom to others. That is the essence of what I want to write and share with the world.

I also realized I wanted to create a movement and build a tribe of people who want to inspire others. I want inspiration to become contagious. I want it to spread like wildfire. I want to bring people together behind a positive purpose. To build each other up. Lift each other up.

We live in a world where fear, stress, and busyness rule the day. That is why we must step back, look to our ancestors and ourselves for what matters.

Throughout history, storytelling has been used to pass on wisdom and inspiration. I believe that we have so many stories of inspiration across all walks of life that aren't considered "newsworthy." That is because society has grossly skewed what is newsworthy. We need to take back our power and strength as a tribe and share inspiring stories.

Join me! Get back to your roots!

Sit with me by the campfire. Grab a cup of coffee or hot cocoa. Get your comfy sofa slippers, that favorite soft sweater, get cozy, and let's share life-giving stories.

As we sit around the campfire, imagine sharing all those stories that have inspired us most. Stories from our own journeys. Stories that provide light in a world where it can often feel quite dark.

The campfire and storytelling traditions that come from our ancestors carry great value. We learn from each other through storytelling. We remember more valuable lessons when shared within the context of a story.

We build connection, tribe, and community through storytelling. We gain new insights and ideas we can apply to our own lives through the story's others share.

In sharing our stories, we heal through vulnerability. We become more aware of our patterns. The more we share and let down our guard, the faster we can heal. Healing comes from sharing in circles.

Take a moment to sit and reflect on your stories. Perhaps even take a moment to jot down some notes or write in your journal.

A BUMPY JOURNEY

In this lifetime, I know it's my calling to help people heal themselves. I also believe that my body and its ailments allow me to reach people in a very real way. I have been coping with chronic pain for most of my life.

Beyond my physical pain, I have also experienced many personal and professional challenges. In my professional life, I climbed the corporate ladder with great success but also experienced frequent layoffs. Sadly, each layoff was coupled with a new health diagnosis or challenge.

At twenty-three, I had ten-level spinal fusion after four to five years of visiting chronic back pain clinics. I lost myself entirely to chronic pain for several years. I survived an extremely abusive marriage and divorce where I nearly lost my identity. I survived a bear charging me in the woods alone, a scorpion sting in Guatemala, a yearlong sinus infection, which led to surgery, a severe concussion, and so much more.

I don't believe most of us experience that much physical turmoil in a single lifetime. After continuing to see the same pattern over and over, I decided to go on a quest to break the cycle.

Believe it or not, that quest is what led to the moment where this book came into existence.

And then, years later, a week after my scorpion sting, I had an epiphany; life was throwing these crazy stories into my path, so I would get the message and write a book already. Clearly, I had a message to share.

Even after hearing the message loud and clear, I started the book but went in the wrong direction again. Over four years have passed since the scorpion epiphany. This time I am dedicated to completing this project because I know it's on the right topic.

During a morning meditation, it came to me. *Instead of focusing on pain and suffering, focus on inspiration and transformation! Share your stories of transformational growth through inspiration.*

I think the reason it took so long to get started is that transformation is a painful process. And sharing your transformation is extremely vulnerable. It's much like baring your soul to a new partner. You never know how they'll receive it, and there's a chance they may reject you entirely.

The reality is that *without* vulnerability, transformation is impossible. The more open and vulnerable you can be, the faster you will grow into who you were meant to be.

I am here to share my experiences and provide tools for transformation because I want to bring health, clarity, and business to you so you can build the life of your dreams.

I want to help you define success on your terms. I want to help you get clear on the legacy you wish to leave behind. I want to help you live an intentional life with *big dreams* on your bucket list. And I want to help you bust through obstacles and fears with love, passion, and knowing.

MY INVITATION TO YOU

If you're ready to join me on this journey of transformation, please read on. Even if you're feeling some resistance, you're in the right place.

What we resist persists . . . it doesn't magically go away on its own.

What we resist is usually what we need to do most to grow and transform.

Press on! I promise you it's worth it. You're worth it!

And I am here to guide you every step of the way.

Your Loving Guide,

Holly Jean Jackson

1

WHY INSPIRATION?

"The only people for me are the mad ones,
the ones who are mad to live,
mad to talk, mad to be saved . . .
the ones who never yawn
and say a commonplace
thinking but burn, burn, burn
like fabulous yellow roman candles
exploding like spiders across the stars."

~ JACK KEROUAC

I am not ready to die! These were the words screaming through my mind as I faced a mamma bear in the middle of the woods all alone.

You see, I had decided to take a backpacking trip alone in the woods of Lassen Volcanic National Park in Northern California. I was working through some things after my divorce, and I was stuck.

I was in a step study for codependency, and I was on the all-too-difficult step of spiritual inventory. For those of you who aren't familiar with Celebrate Recovery and step studies, here's how it works.

You choose a problem you're working on and attend a group session where you share openly the challenges you're facing. It's extremely vulnerable and yet also very healing. After my divorce, I knew my part in what went wrong was that I was codependent. I wanted to work on it so I wouldn't repeat it in future relationships. My relationship had been extremely abusive, so I was very motivated to change.

The spiritual inventory step involves writing out every single thing you have done wrong toward others, what you could have done differently, and how you have forgiven that wrongdoing. It also includes an inventory of every wrongdoing others have done against you, your reflections and lessons learned from that, and how you're moving forward.

As you might guess, it's a painful process. I was feeling a lot of resistance. So, I decided to do something else. I was excited and yet a little scared. Regardless, I chose to go on a backpacking trip alone. I wanted to make it a fun experience and remove any distractions so I could get it done.

On the first day, I found myself hiking through a lot of burnt-down forest. It was sad to see all that the fires had destroyed. But I could also see new growth. New life. As I continued to hike, I saw so many beautiful lakes. Given how this inventory would require a great deal of self-reflection, I began looking at the lakes like mirrors. It felt like I was in exactly the right place at the right moment.

I stopped for lunch on a stunning lake. I pressed on to my first night's campsite on another magical lake. That first night, other people were camping around me, but not many—only a few small groups and couples. My biggest fear, going backpacking alone, was being alone. Alone with myself and alone with my anxious thoughts and mind chatter. I was worried I couldn't handle it and wouldn't have an escape.

I needed to face the fear head-on to feel like I was whole again. I could handle anything life threw at me. So, I chose a campsite away from the others to experience it. And you know what? It wasn't bad. In fact, I finally got started on my inventory. And because there weren't any distractions, it was easy.

The next morning, I got up and made coffee and breakfast. Then I pressed on. I had a thirty-five-mile loop planned for my three-day quest with many lakes and mountains to see and explore.

Day two was even more stunning. I had made it past the edge of where the fire occurred and was in a luscious forest with deep greens all around. The lakes in that part of the park were even more stunning as the water reflected shades of green from the healthy trees.

"Thank you, God!" I soaked up the beauty and was so grateful I made the trip. It was exactly what I needed. As I hiked on, I realized I hadn't seen another human all day long. At first, it felt a little alarming. But as I pressed on, I realized how much I enjoyed being deep in nature alone. It's an entirely different experience. You see more, hear more, smell more, and feel more.

Sitting by the lake, I could feel the gentle breeze brushing against my face. I could smell the fresh dew on the ground—that fresh morning scent where you can smell the greenery around you, alive and magnificent—the silence of nature. Only the chirping of birds letting you know it's the start of a new day. The light rustling of trees as they sway in the breeze, dancing to nature's rhythm.

As I watched the sunrise, I saw the beautiful shimmer and reflection of light across the stillness of the lake. The reflection created a stunning mirror of the world. I could see the trees reflected in the still lake. And when I leaned over, I could see myself.

Sitting back down, I thought to myself . . .

I feel so much more grounded, clear, and peaceful. Nature is so healing and perfect. I can breathe again. I feel at home. It feels as if God or the universe is giving me a huge hug, reminding me that this is where I need to come to feel safe and at home. My senses are heightened.

I love that I can enjoy silence and solitude. I can work on healing from within in this space. Getting away from the noise of the world is so essential to true healing. Now, I can really dig in and get to the root of what I need to transform and heal. I must do this more often. I must keep this in my arsenal for healing.

I highly recommend forest bathing, hiking, or backpacking solo in nature if you love the outdoors. Give it a try. See what it opens in your world.

As I pressed on to my second campsite, I came across an even more beautiful lake. I found the perfect spot near the lake to set up camp. After setting up, I decided to read and journal a bit more while having a small snack. I can't describe how grateful I was to be in that amazing location alone.

After a bit, I noticed a group of guys had set up camp way down on the other side of the lake. A little bit later, one of them began shouting at me. I thought they were saying hello, so I called "Hello" back. They continued shouting something, but I still couldn't hear. So, I said, "I'll come over and say hi in a little bit."

But they shouted once more, and that time, I heard them. My heart stopped. He shouted, "Lady, there's a bear near your camp!"

I looked to my right at the sandbank strip less than a quarter-mile from me. Sure enough, there was a big cinnamon mamma bear. She hadn't seen me yet.

I left all my things and very slowly and carefully backed my way over to the guy's campsite. I said, "Thank you so much! Can you please help me go over to get my things from my campsite? I can't do it alone. I know we need to make a lot of noise and stick together in a group for safety."

"I'll help you," one of the guys said. We gathered pots and pans to make noise and went to my site. As we banged and clattered our way to the site, he explained to me that the bear was unusual. "This bear is acting strange," the guy said. "It tried to attack me and the group yesterday. We had to charge her back to get to our destination. I think it's because of the drought, but we should be extra careful, and you should camp near us tonight to be safe."

I thanked him and said it was a good plan. We gathered my things, and I set up camp near them. That group of guys was the best group I could have run into. The gentleman who helped me was the former mayor of Citrus Heights (a city outside of Sacramento, California). Another gentleman was a retired highway patrolman. Another was writing a book. You get the idea. Those guys were really sweet, kind, and experienced backpackers.

They were on day three of a two-week trip. As we shared stories, they shared their Cuban cigars and high-end whiskey. It was like finding heaven in the middle of the woods. It was a serendipitous and magical experience.

I took my cigar and walked to the lakeside and began working on my inventory once again. The guys knew when to give me and each other space. It was a perfect balance. Around dinner time, we sat together and shared stories of life and adventure. It was a fun bonding experience—the way I think we were intended to live as humans, a way of life we have sadly gotten away from with modern life and technology.

The next morning, over coffee, the guys shared with me some bear pointers, including how to charge a bear. They also gave me a whistle in case I needed to alert others that I was in danger. The former mayor gave me a pin from his election campaign that I put on my hat for good luck. Then we parted ways as they continued deeper into the park while I headed back to my car.

As I hiked alone, I remember feeling rejuvenated, energized, and thrilled with life.

What a great adventure. What perfect serendipity that I would meet such kindred spirits in the forest. I reflected on my spiritual inventory, which I had finally completed. I felt such incredible peace at facing my demons and offering forgiveness. I had made a full account of all wrongs against me and started the path of ongoing forgiveness. I also made a full list of all the wrongdoings I did towards others and began the process of forgiving myself, reflecting on what triggered the wrong action and how I could mend relationships I wanted to restore.

I continued to soak up the gratitude and peace like I had never experienced in my entire lifetime.

As I pressed on, the forest became more luscious and thick. Everything was so green. I could almost feel it vibrating. Full of life. Full of untapped energy and vitality. It was beautiful beyond words. *Amazing . . . the forest went from burnt shambles to something stunning.*

Then, I glanced down and noticed some fresh bear paw prints. And another set. One was large, and the other was small. I realized in a panic why the bear was acting so strange. She was a mom in a drought trying to protect her cub. We were simply in the wrong place at the wrong time. It all made sense.

Then, I began to panic as I realized I was really in the wrong place.

God, please let these paw prints be older than they appear. Please protect me and keep me safe. I have already been hiking for three hours. I am not anywhere close to my group. I am not anywhere close to finishing my hike. I haven't seen another soul all day. I haven't heard humans since I left camp this morning. I am completely alone.

I turned the next corner, and there was a mamma bear. I didn't see her cub . . . I hoped she didn't see me. But immediately, she began charging towards me.

Terror shook through my entire body. I had never experienced that level of fear. That much adrenaline, charging through my body. My entire life flashed before my eyes. I could see everything from my life in an instant.

Thank goodness I journaled forgiveness and asked for forgiveness for my wrongdoings. I feel surprisingly peaceful at this moment. Everything feels very still. But wait, I don't want to die! I didn't come out here to die. I came out here to transform, to grow. To live my life more fully.

Okay, Holly, what did the guys tell you? They said stand your ground. Make yourself big. Make noise. Let's do that.

I stood my ground, made myself big, made noise. It didn't work.

Okay, that didn't work. I really don't want to die. I have so much more I want to do. So much I want to share with the world. So many people I want to forgive. I am so angry! This is not how things are supposed to end!

Those guys showed me how to charge the bear. Let's give that a try.

I took all the anger and passion inside me and took one step forward and shouted at the bear—charging her!

It worked! She stopped, looked at me, a bit stunned. And I thought to myself, *Holy crap! It worked. Thank goodness. Thank you, God! I am so grateful to be alive.*

But it was short-lived. She then stood on two feet growling and snarling and then went back down on all fours and charged me once again—closing the gap between us even further. That time, as my life flashed before my eyes, I thought to myself, *if I do die, make it fast. I don't want to be out here bleeding out for days. Nor do I want to live a life as a mauled bear survivor, disfigured and shambled for life.* Eerie, but that's what I was thinking.

Then, I got angry once again. *Hey, I didn't come out here to be bear food. I just got some real peace and clarity for my life. I am not ready to throw that away and die. I am not here to be bear food.* So, I stood my ground, made myself large again, took a step forward, and charged with everything in my being!

It probably sounded like two bears fighting in the woods. The sounds you make when you want to survive are very guttural and instinctual.

It worked! She stopped, really stunned that time. She began to walk away from me with disinterest. I continued to stand my ground as she left for what felt like forever. Eventually, when I felt like she was gone, I began to run, and I didn't stop running until I saw people.

At that point, I felt like I was safe and could let my guard down. I realized I had survived coming face-to-face with a charging bear in the woods. *Crazy! I can't believe it! I want to call all the people I need to ask forgiveness from. I want to shout my gratitude from the treetops. I want to share my story with others because I feel so ignited and inspired. So alive! I have another shot at doing life in a new way. I am so lucky.*

Later, I realized a lot of fears in my life weren't all too scary.

You see, I was allowing fear to drive my life. I wasn't making good decisions, often living in indecision due to fear. For example, I used to be afraid of riding my bike in the wind when it was strong for fear it would knock me over or into a car on the road.

After that experience, I wasn't afraid anymore. I had faced one of the scariest things ever. Not only did I face a charging bear in the woods and survive it alone, but I faced my own anxious thinking. I faced my inner chatter, and it wasn't all bad. *Now, I know I can do anything and face anything. I feel lighter, excited, and empowered.*

Now, every time I share this story, I see others lean in and light up. And yeah, it's a great story.

But the reason they lean in and light up is that they can see themselves in the story. They want inner peace. They want to face themselves, so they have confidence and a firm foundation to face and thrive in life. They want to have an amazing story to share with others. To inspire others.

Here's the thing; if I can face a bear head on alone, there is no fear too big in your life you can't C-H-A-R-G-E head on!

You heard that right. You can face any fear in your life. It's possible.

Perhaps your bear is leaving an abusive relationship. Or perhaps your bear is starting your own business. Or perhaps your bear is making a change in your personal life. Regardless of what your bear is, I am here to tell you; you can face it head-on. You have the power.

And guess what, there is freedom in that. When we face our fears head-on, we experience freedom. We experience clarity, and we experience life in a way that allows us to soar and thrive at a new level.

So, what's stopping you? Are you ready to get inspired? Are you ready to transform your life and health?

I am here to share powerful stories of inspiration and transformation. Stories going from pain to thriving. From struggle to surrender and freedom. From hopeless to inspired. These tools will help you build a step-by-step plan to improve your health starting today.

But first, let's start by exploring inspiration.

What is it that causes this spark within us? It's that moment where we realize something inside of us has forever changed. And yet, if we don't take action, nothing has really changed at all.

It's an allusive, intangible feeling inside. It's extremely personal, and there is no one size fits all definition for it.

Why is inspiration the premise for this book series? Why is it the foundation for a lot of what we will explore?

Inspiration is the spark inside that ignites something new. It's the seed of an idea. The spark of creation. To make change. To take action.

Inspiration is where I believe every single invention, idea, book, hypothesis, and vision stems from.

It could come from a moment of clarity during meditation. It might come to you during a walk, run, or hike. It may even happen when you least expect it—while you're in the shower or doing some menial day-to-day task.

For some, inspiration comes from hearing stories from a friend, or a mentor, or a speaker on stage, or through a book. Sometimes, we need to see ourselves in someone else's story to get that internal spark.

And the stories that inspire us don't have to be wild, extreme, or huge. Sometimes, the most ordinary of stories can spark that flame within us. We see ourselves in that person's story, and we want the change that they experienced.

I hear this time and time again. The age-old story of climbing the corporate ladder only to realize that it didn't lead to happiness. I experienced that as well. I thought that achieving success at the top in my career would make me happier. More successful. More financially secure. And yet, I kept finding myself in a pattern. Stuck in a loop.

You see, I kept getting laid off, and every time, I also experienced a massive health challenge. After one layoff, I experienced a massive concussion that took me a year to recover from. During another one, I had a sinus infection that lasted a year, leading to a tonsillectomy.

After the fourth layoff, I saw the pattern. I knew I had to break the cycle. I didn't want to live that way anymore.

While I was working a new corporate job, I began exploring my options. I had consulted on the side part-time for years, but I didn't just want to start a consulting agency. I had been career coaching for years, but I didn't love doing that.

At my yoga teacher training a year earlier, I had heard about coaching. I found myself drawn to it. I had always coached my friends and colleagues on their health for free. It was just a passion I had. I really cared about optimizing health and performance.

So, I decided to get certified as a health coach. Once I dove into the curriculum, I decided to also get certified as a life coach, and then transformational coaching method, and then mastery. I went deep into the coaching field. I found it fascinating and personally transformational in a way I had never experienced. The transformational coaching method allows you to learn how to uncover behaviors you want to shift. You learn how to uncover and shift beliefs and identity.

Can you imagine changing your limiting beliefs? Changing your identity (the bits that need an upgrade)?

It's powerful, life-changing stuff!

Then, I decided to begin stretching my entrepreneurial spirit. I began to offer my friends health coaching at a heavily discounted rate. I needed practice, and I needed testimonials from clients.

I took on five clients my first year while I was still completing my training. I loved it! But I also knew health wasn't the whole thing. I wanted to help people break the cycle like I did. I wanted to offer them the whole package. I wanted them to see that they could leave the corporate world and create a business and life they could thrive in.

So, I started my holistic business coaching company to help others heal their lives and build businesses to help others in the process. And, because I am deeply passionate about health and wellness, I decided to work with business owners in that space.

People ask me if it was scary to leave the corporate world. And yes, in some ways, it was. It was all new territory. And when you go into business, you're constantly learning new skills because you start out doing everything as a solopreneur. To some, that is overwhelming. For me, it was invigorating!

It would have been scarier if I didn't have financial support and work to get started. For the first six months, I was still working full time. After that, I asked around through my network for a part-time consulting job. I only wanted to work twenty to thirty hours but replace most of my previous salary to free up my time to build the business. I emailed twenty people. I got five responses. Two of them were viable leads, and ultimately, one led to an opportunity that supported my business over the first year.

When you really want something, there's not just one path forward. There are so many options. And the more creative you get, the more possibilities you uncover. And when you tap into your network and community and ask for exactly what you want, you usually get just that. I was even honest about building my business with my new employer. And they still wanted to hire me because I had value to offer.

If you're reading or listening to this and you're sick of your job and dread going to work every day, I am here to tell you; there is another way. There is hope. There are other possibilities. It's possible to live a healthy life and have a thriving business. It's possible to love every aspect of your life. It's possible to be free.

I hope this ignites a spark within you. A light that you can't turn away from. If you feel that right now, pause and sit with your eyes closed for a moment and let that light and spark grow. Give it space and power every single morning and throughout the day. Let it grow. Listen to it. Allow it to be your guide and inner compass.

Do this, and you will be on to the secret of life . . . following your passion!

When we listen to our inspiration and passion, we can do no wrong. And even when the journey hits roadblocks or speed bumps, or massive failures, you will still be happy. Because you're living your life full out. You're on the journey to defining and building success on your own terms. When you follow your passion, you realize that your journey is your journey.

Comparing yourself to others is pointless. Because what you want is specific to who you are, and no one else is like you. No one else can provide the superhero powers and ninja skills you hold within you. So why not listen to that inner spark and take action?

Take one small step toward exactly what you want. One small step toward freedom, peace, and happiness.

Don't wait another single day. It's too easy to let a moment of inspiration get away. When we don't take immediate action, we allow life to get in the way. And then a day, a week, a month, years pass us by. And we reflect back a decade later, wondering what happened. How did we miss out on that idea?

Don't make that mistake. Instead, take action today. Even if it's the smallest of steps forward, do something to move forward.

I believe that inspiration is the seed of an idea with a charge of energy behind it that, when we take action, becomes the roots and foundation of something amazing. Inspiration is the fuel that starts the creation process. It allows us to tap into something bigger than ourselves. It creates a spark of energy within that forces us to examine what we do next. It encourages us to take action or make a change or re-evaluate life. It's the fuel we need to create motivation. To spark change.

And while inspiration is that moment of ignition where we could create something astounding, why is it that so many of us doubt it? Why is it that when we are hit with such an incredible, clearly wonderful idea, we continue with life as is?

I believe it's because too many of us let fear get in the way. We are so comfortable with the status quo that we fear any ideas that might change life as we know it. We are stuck in our ways.

YOU ARE THE ONLY THING GETTING IN THE WAY OF YOUR SUCCESS AND CRAZY MIRACLES BEYOND YOUR WILDEST DREAMS!

Some of us don't let fear block us but think that if we sit back and visualize our inspiring idea, it will magically burst into existence. And guess what, that isn't how it works. Inspiration gives us the idea or that burst of energy to do something new. To take action. To transform and change. But it does require that we take bold action that matches the size of our ideas and dreams.

So, while mindset is important, it's not everything. When my clients are taking big action that matches the size of their dreams, and we don't see the results we should, it's time to look at mindset, beliefs, and identity.

Until you start taking *bold* action, stop using mindset as an excuse.

Yes, you heard me. Too many people use mindset and visualization as their excuse for not succeeding. They think they can visualize it into existence. And while I am a *huge* proponent of visualization and mindset, it's not everything you need. There are so many other practical things you need to succeed.

You must take action. And sometimes, that may mean you make mistakes. It may mean embarrassment. It may even mean you fall flat on your face.

When you take action, at least you aren't living in regret. You aren't in the victim mindset where you blame others for your failures. Because you are living full out and taking action towards what you want to create in life.

If you take nothing away from this book, I hope you walk away with at least this: *Take action today.*

Take at least one small step closer to what you desire. A goal. An idea. A change. A transformation. Commit to it and grow 1% closer to that goal every single day.

That is how we build momentum. Momentum leads to discipline and commitment. But no one can do it for you. Fixing unhealthy habits doesn't happen overnight. It requires commitment to the goals you have set for yourself. Businesses aren't created without dedication to an idea and a vision.

BUILDING THE LIFE AND BUSINESS OF YOUR DREAMS REQUIRES COMMITMENT, PASSION, AND ACTION.

If that is something you desire, I encourage you to build your foundation. And your foundation starts with having a strong health toolkit.

Looking for more inspiration?

Check out my Inspiration Contagion Podcast on your favorite podcast player or by visiting: http://www.inspirationcontagion.com/

I have interviewed hundreds of inspiring leaders who have amazing stories to share.

Each of them has faced challenges. Each of them has struggled. And yet, they have chosen inspiration.

They have chosen the path less traveled. To be a light in this world. To face fear head-on. To be an inspiration to others.

2

INSPIRATION APPLIED

"Great things are done when men and mountains meet."

~ WILLIAM BLAKE

If inspiration is the ignition and fuel to success, then let's dig into how you can tap into inspiration today. Inspiration applied means we are now building the roadmap and steps that you must take to find your own inspiration, how to stay inspired, how to tap into your passion and power within, and so much more.

Okay, let's get clear on what you want, which is one of the keys to inspiration.

FIND YOUR INSPIRATION

Inspiration is the ignition and fuel that allows us to transform and commit to making change and transformation in every aspect of our life that will stick. Inspiration is what ignites the motivation to take daily action that creates huge change. It's what allows us to make a massive impact (the ripple effect) on those around us. Inspiration is what will enable us to change the world.

REFLECTION QUESTIONS

So, if you lack inspiration, how do you find it? Start by reflecting and journaling on the following questions:

1. What books or movies left a lasting impression on you or inspired you most?

   a. What childhood books or movies do you love most, and why?

   b. Are there any similarities across the books or movies you love (i.e., hero's journey, love story, etc.)?

   c. What about each of them inspired you and why?

2. Who has inspired you?

   a. A speaker you saw?

   b. A song you heard?

   c. An actor you felt moved by?

   d. A mentor who changed your world?

   e. What about those individuals inspired you and why?

3. What places inspire you most?

   a. Do you love the sound of waves on the beach?

   b. Are you moved by mountains and hikes in the woods?

   c. Does being near animals inspire you (i.e., the zoo, sanctuaries, nature)?

   d. Do you love the sound of a bustling city with loads of people?

   e. What place brings you the most peace and energy in the world?

   f. What about those places inspire you and why?

4. What moments or experiences inspire you?

   a. Do sentimental moments (i.e., reflecting back on graduation, an anniversary, etc.) inspire you?

   b. Do moments of quiet and aloneness (i.e., meditation, a solo walk or hike) inspire you?

   c. Do moments full of exhilaration (i.e., roller coasters, skydiving, rock climbing, etc.) inspire you?

   d. What moments leave a lasting and energizing impression on you?

   e. What about those moments inspire you and why?

Your job over the next week is to become an expert on inspiration. I want to challenge you to get ultra-curious. Experiment, play and have fun with this. Tune in to what moments, experiences, people, places, smells, etc., inspire you. Write it down. Reflect on it.

Our goal this week is to become experts on what inspires us so we can tap into it when we need to. We are building your inspiration toolkit.

Take copious notes, ask others what inspires them, explore, experiment, and most importantly, have fun! You've got this!

For those of you who are still feeling lost, here are some examples of what inspires me:

- Sunrises and sunsets
- Backpacking or hiking in the mountains
- Stories of transformation, struggle, and growth
- Other business owner's success stories
- Music with personal stories of love or transformation
- Playing piano or singing
- Watching a symphony, opera, ballet, or orchestra perform
- Bookstores—I love visiting libraries and bookstores because of all the incredible stories that are waiting for me to discover
- Coffee Shops—the hustle and bustle and just knowing that some people in those shops are writing novels or other books inspires me

Moments of Inspiration:

- first kiss
- falling in love
- starting my business
- leaving corporate
- skydiving
- my divorce
- graduating from Celebrate Recovery
- traveling (any form of travel but especially international and experiencing new cultures)
- saying I love you the first time
- deciding to start a family
- facing the bear in the woods
- meeting my nephews for the first time
- moving back to North Carolina
- moving to California
- my first solo backpacking trip
- getting to pet a wombat in Australia
- holding a koala
- spending time with friends
- cooking dinner with loved ones
- sharing a meal with loved ones
- laughing at anything
- making others smile and laugh.

Speakers and People:

Seeing Sean Stephenson speak on stage and share his story and struggle but how he still sticks to his passion and quest, or Catherine Hoke sharing about prisoners and helping them reintegrate into society and how they're just like us—human. There are so many touching speeches I have heard—too many to list.

- Brene Brown
- Tim Ferris
- my family
- J.K Rowling
- Gabrielle Bernstein
- Louis Hay
- Marianne Williamson
- Philip Pullman
- James Patterson
- Stephen King
- Elon Musk

Hopefully, you're starting to refine your list of what, who, where, and how you're most inspired. As you become more aware, you'll notice it's easier to be grateful for what you have in your life. It's also easier to tap into inspiration even on days when things aren't going your way.

And that's the whole idea. We want to stay in that flow of inspired energy where the best ideas and creations stem from. So now that you understand your form of inspiration, let's dive into internal inspiration and how to ignite your passion!

Need some extra help? Check out the Inspiration Worksheet here: https://coachhollyjackson.activehosted.com/f/52

INTERNAL INSPIRATION AND YOUR PASSION

A lot of what we described above is about external forms of inspiration. How do we tap into our internal inspiration?

The more we know about what inspires us, the easier it is to know the energy and feeling of inspiration. Once we are more familiar with that, we can begin to play with our internal energy.

As you tune into your external inspirations, reflect on why they inspire you. What parts of your body you feel it in (i.e., is it in your heart center, your third eye, your gut?)

Let's dig into your passion as well. Passion is when you have defined your internal inspiration in a very personal way. Your passion is the fire behind the actions you must take to achieve your lofty goals. It's what gets you out of bed even when your body rages against you. It's what fuels you when everyone around you says it's impossible. It's your guide and compass through darkness, confusion, fear, and overwhelm. It's your constant true north.

That is why we *must* define our passion. We can't allow others to tell us what we want from life. When we do, we are doomed to a life of misery, pain, and unhappiness.

You deserve a life of inspiration, passion, joy, and excitement!

Let's dive in so you can get clear on your internal inspiration and passion today!

Here are some questions for you to reflect on as you begin to explore your internal inspiration and what lights you up (i.e., your passion). I encourage you to reflect and journal on these, close your eyes, meditate, and visualize the responses to each question. Visualization is a powerful way of gaining clarity on internal desires, passions, and inspiration.

Internal Inspiration and Passion Questions:

- What does inspiration feel like to you?
- Where do you feel it in your body?
- What's the significance of where you feel it in your body?
- Is it in different parts of the body for various forms of inspiration?
- What color does your inspiration take on if you close your eyes and imagine seeing it?

- What sensations does your inspiration provide (i.e., does it heighten what you feel, see, smell; does it make you tingly, energized, happy)?
- When you feel inspired, what do you want to do with that (i.e., does it make you want to take action, move, do something)?
- What are you most passionate about?
- What's the legacy you wish to leave behind?
- What lights you up inside?
- Can you expand that sensation or energy to feel it in your entire body?
- Can you begin to tap into that inspiration at any time, any place, anywhere?

As you explore these questions, don't judge what comes up. Remain open and curious. Have fun with it and take your time. There is no point in rushing this exploration. The better you know your internal inspiration and define your passion, the easier it will be to grow and change.

A Note of Caution: You may not want to share what's coming up for you. Sometimes, when we begin a big transformation, and others aren't ready, they'll try to bring us down. Right now, we want to expand our inspiration muscle. Don't let others dampen your light as you explore.

Feeling Stuck?

Using visualization is a powerful way to get unstuck. I have created a guided visualization specifically geared to helping you uncover your internal inspiration. It will walk you through these questions and more.

To get the most out of this visualization, I encourage you to use it daily for at least twenty days. Be sure to keep a journal or notepad close by to write down what comes up each day.

Download a copy of the visualization here: https://coachhollyjackson.activehosted.com/f/36

You can also download the Passion Worksheet here: https://coachhollyjackson.activehosted.com/f/52

Once you have developed the vision for your health and life, it's important to hold that vision—continue to breathe life into it.

WHAT WE FOCUS ON GROWS. MAKE SURE YOU'RE FOCUSING ON
WHAT YOU WANT TO GROW AND WHAT YOU WANT TO TRANSFORM.

If you're struggling to hold your vision, check out my Holding a Vision Worksheet here: https://coachhollyjackson.activehosted.com/f/40

If you didn't read chapter one and explore what inspires you, be sure to start there. The clearer you are on what inspires you and being able to tap into that feeling or that energy, the more you'll get out of this experience.

DEFINE SUCCESS ON YOUR TERMS

Too many of us allow others to define success for us. It could be a teacher, a mentor, a parent, or a boss. And even more of us don't have a definition for success at all. We have no idea what we believe is successful.

While I was climbing the corporate ladder I thought success was getting that next promotion. I believed hitting six figures and getting that next bonus would make me happy. The reality is that the further up the ladder I climbed, the less happy I was. I felt more pressure, stress, and busy. I didn't feel fulfilled or satisfied. If anything, it felt like life was stealing my energy.

With each challenge and setback I've continued to fine tune my definition of success. After leaving my husband and going through the process of divorce I began exploring what success meant to me for the first time. I no longer had someone else trying to define it for me. My ex husband looked at success in a very material way. He valued anything that showed status—a fancy car, an executive job title, brand name clothing, etc.

Getting away from this simplistic view of success, I was now more open to exploring new possibilities. I began viewing success during this period of my life as being able to survive on my own two feet. You see, I had come to believe that I couldn't make it on my own. Because I was in such a verbally abusive relationship, I was led to believe I was incapable and depended on him for everything from taxes to fixing something simple in the house.

When I was on my own at last, I found that doing my taxes was quite simple and I enjoyed doing it. With each small step I took, I felt more empowered. Building a new piece of furniture I ordered felt like a huge accomplishment. Getting a new job, finding a new place to live, moving, joining a church, teaching children's ministry, etc.—the more I took action independently, the better I felt.

I felt like I could do anything!

When I experienced my concussion, I re-evaluated my definition of success again. When major changes in life happen, it's a great opportunity to re-examine values, priorities and our definition of success. While healing from that concussion, I found my definition for success was very simple. I wanted to be whole and to heal myself again. I wanted to be able to live a simple life, stress free. I didn't want to lose my identity to the injury. I didn't want to live in fear or limitation.

Because it took me a year to recover, I learned how to celebrate baby steps and small wins. Being able to spend an afternoon with a friend was a *big* win for me back then. Having a day free from a migraine and nausea was amazing.

I also learned how to be patient. Patience has not been my virtue but having this time to slow down was invaluable. I learned how to work on my anxiety and stress. During this year of healing, my values and priorities were quite different. Health was my top priority. Taking care of me came first.

Today I look at success quite differently. A successful day for me is one where I start my day in meditation. I tap into my own energy and inspiration. I visualize my long-term goals and what I'm creating in the world. Then I start working on whatever is my top priority that day.

If I'm not feeling well, I flex my time to take care of me. If I have a friend or client in need, I shift my schedule to be of service. For me, success is about being of service to others and helping people uncover and achieve their dreams and goals. It's about listening to my body for continued healing and growth and continually remaining dedicated to learning. It's about always being coachable and deeply being present—listening from a space of non-judgment. It's about saying yes to what's important to me and no to what's out of alignment.

I like to reflect on each day in the evening to see how I did. Did I have what I define as a successful day? If not, what could I have done better? Has my definition of success changed somehow? This keeps me on track. I have more productive and invigorating days when I stay tuned into my internal guidance for personal success.

When you don't know what success looks like, how will you know that you achieved it? When will you know it's time to celebrate? How will you say no to the wrong things that will get in your way and yes to the right things that will accelerate your momentum?

The answer is *you won't*. You'll bounce from idea to idea, job to job, failure to failure. It will feel like you're stuck on a hamster wheel, going nowhere. And that's because it's going nowhere.

What's the point of your life, your actions, and your journey if you have no idea what you're trying to build?

Now that you're clear on your internal inspiration and your passion, it's time to map out your definition of personal success very clearly. I don't mean external success (i.e., money, fancy car, retirement, etc.). I mean, what does success feel like, look like, and what is the legacy you're building to leave behind.

You can also use definitions of success for various aspects of your life. For example, you can determine what a successful day looks like, what a successful year looks like, what a successful career or business looks like. You get the point.

But for now, I want you to work on what success looks like for your life. When you die, what do you want people to remember about you?

Here are some questions for you to work on to get your juices and ideas flowing:

- What do you value most in your life (i.e., family, travel, freedom, fun)?
- What does success look like for each of the top five things you value (i.e., if you value your family, does success mean building deep, trusting relationships with family or spending a lot of quality time together)?
- How would the people who know you best today describe you, your character, and your life purpose?
- How do you want those people to describe you—is there a difference or a gap?
- When you die, what do you hope people will say about you?

- What is the legacy you wish to leave behind for your children or the next generation (i.e., what do you want to be remembered for; choose one core thing)?
- What is your goal one year from today? Ten years from today?
- What would you need to do to change those goals to make them so exciting that no matter what, you woke up with excitement, ready to jump out of bed and get started?
- Are your goals big enough? Exciting enough? Will they stretch you and force you to grow?
- When you look at your goals for the next year or your ten-year goal, what are the three things at the core of success for you (i.e., impacting people, helping people, teaching, inspiring, helping business owners)?
- What is your definition of personal success?

Be sure to take your time working through these questions. Reflect on them. Ask loved ones what they see in you.

Get curious about what would really light you up inside. Visualize your funeral and how you want to be remembered. Meditate on these. Try new things if you still aren't clear on what you're most passionate about.

Our definition of success will change over our lifetime. It is something you should revisit once a year to check in and make sure it still reflects your values and goals. If not, go through those questions once again until you have your personal definition for success.

Now that you have your definition, check in with it every day. Every decision you make should be taking you closer to success. It should align with your values. It should make things easier in the long run. And if it's something that's not aligned with your success goals, then say *no*. Otherwise, you'll be forced to say *no* to important things that will move you closer to your goals. It will slow your momentum.

Recently, I read in a book or heard on a podcast that when people say they're busy, it's an indicator that their life is out of control. Busy people are people who haven't stopped to define success for themselves, and so, they're saying yes to everything, hoping they'll somehow find happiness along the way.

In contrast, when you're clear on what you're building, what success is, and what your goals are, then you shouldn't be busy. You should be focused. You should be getting things done that are building your momentum. You should be in flow, receiving opportunities for growth, teachers in the right moments, and seeing new possibilities that will make your journey even better or easier.

When I went through the certification programs to become a health coach and life coach, I realized I had been doing so many things all wrong. I was focusing my time on the wrong things. And I kept finding myself backed into a corner.

I could feel my anxiety and overwhelm. My shoulders and neck tensed. My mind raced with all the things on my to do list. I found myself holding my breath or hyperventilating. I was panicking. Because I had overcommitted my time. I made myself "busy." And with all the wrong stuff.

This kept happening all the time. I would be so overwhelmed by my schedule or my to-do list that I would go into a frenzy. Sometimes it would even cause panic attacks or migraines.

Once I realized this was a pattern, I began unwinding it.

As I reflected on how I got here, I went back to face things from my childhood that were haunting me. Things like my limiting beliefs, including: *There's something wrong with me, or I'm too much, or bad things happen to me.* What many of these messages had in common were that I wanted to make people around me happy. But in doing so I wasn't happy.

And when I looked at the list of things I committed to doing, most of it was to please others. None of it was what I wanted or aligned with my goals or priorities.

So I decided I wanted to build out my own roadmap forward—my own compass so to speak. This is how I came up with one of my proprietary tools I use with clients called My Life and Business Compass. I built this tool to stop backing myself into a corner.

By defining my five life priorities and my top three business goals each quarter, I could see what I needed to say yes to and what I must say no to. I also wrote out my long-term goal and vision for my life to keep me inspired and motivated. Having that there allows me to say no to things that aren't aligned even when it feels hard.

One of my top priorities is my health which includes taking excellent care of myself. I also prioritize my relationships, especially with my friends, family, and partner. Spiritual growth and introspection is always a priority for me. Without continual reflection, there is no growth. Ultimately, we have everything we need inside of us. We just need to stop and listen. Freedom, travel, and new adventures are other priorities that are near and dear to my heart. They allow me to learn, grow, and tap into creativity more readily. I would never sacrifice this priority for anything in the world. Last, but not least, my fifth priority is to help health and wellness business owners reach more people so we can heal more people in the world. In helping heal others, it's my hope that we spread light in the darkness and inspiration instead of fear.

When you understand your priorities and goals, you know what road you're on. It becomes clear what action you need to take next. When faced with a fork in the road, all you need to do is pull out your compass. Ask yourself, which direction will get me closer to what's important to me? Which direction will help me reach my long-term goals? And then take the pathway forward. Only YOU know the answer to which pathway to take. Because only you can define what's important for your life's journey.

Take the time, do the work. It's worth it. You're worth it. Never say you are too busy again.

I have given you the tools and roadmap to take back control of your life, so make sure you use them and start taking the right actions for your path to success. There is no reason for you to be too busy. No reason for you to be unhappy. No reason for you to limit your possibilities.

You can do anything you set your mind to. It starts with knowing what you want and taking small tangible steps towards making it a reality.

INSPIRATION AND YOUR HEALTH

So, what does all of this have to do with your health?

Without health, you won't have the energy or clarity to go after what you desire in this life. Without your health, you won't be able to concentrate on building the life and business of your dreams. Without solid health foundations and tools, you won't know what to do when things go wrong on your journey—when you're faced with stressors, a challenge, or even a pandemic.

HAVING AND MAINTAINING GOOD HEALTH IS THE FOUNDATION TO EVERYTHING.

If we go back in time and look at Abraham Maslow's hierarchy of needs, it starts with food, water, and shelter (physiological needs), then safety. So, as you can see, our needs start with being healthy.

That means reducing pain, getting more energy, optimizing our sleep, eating foods that make us feel good, exercising and making movement a core part of our day, and learning how to cope with stress and anxiety.

When we are in chronic pain, it's difficult to find inspiration. We are so consumed by our pain that we can't see or feel anything else. The pain takes over as the focal point of our life. And that can apply to lots of things outside of pain, like food, alcohol, sex, gambling, and even exercise. We need to remove our pain and addictions in order to free ourselves to experience inspiration, get clear on success, and start making it happen.

If you're feeling hopeless as you read this because you've had pain or addiction for so many years or decades, I want to share a story that may provide you with a glimmer of hope.

By the age of twenty-three, I had struggled with back pain for eight years and had worked with a number of pain clinics and pain experts for over four years. No one could figure out what was causing my pain.

And then, I met a doctor. Dr. Hey told me, "Holly we have reviewed all your x-rays and medical history. It's clear to me that you have degenerative disc disease. What this means is that your spine is aging more rapidly than a healthy spine. You have at least ten compressed discs in your upper spine. To get rid of the constant nerve pain you are experiencing, you need to have surgery. What we need to do is correct the curve of your spine. Right now you have a 72-degree curve. A normal spine has a resting curvature of 30 degrees. We want to go in and fuse ten levels of your spine and fix it at a 30 degree angle. This should get rid of most of your pain."

At the age of twenty-three, my spine looked like that of someone in their eighties. I had a seventy-two-degree hunching forward posture. My parents always thought I simply had bad posture. My mom would say, "Holly stop slouching. Sit up straight. Be proud of your body." I would say, "Mom, I am sitting up as straight as I can. I promise. Please stop yelling at me. I am doing my best." But in reality, my spine was failing, lurching me forward, and had created insufferable nerve pain for years.

After years of not knowing what was wrong, I felt relief and excitement that there was finally an answer and finally a solution. Little did I know that I had a long journey ahead of me.

I went through with the procedure two months later. It was less than a year after I got married. It's an extensive surgery. I was under general anesthesia for over four hours. They had to break my spine and put it back together in the correct position (taking it from a seventy-two-degree curve to thirty) with metal screws and two titanium rods.

When I woke up, it was excruciatingly painful. As I woke up it felt like I had rods in my spine. And while I did, feeling that is a lot different than having it described. I felt pain radiating all over my body. I felt stiff and rigid. As I woke up, I was groggy and confused. I felt scared. As I panicked, I thought, *something terrible has happened. Was I in a terrible car accident or something? Maybe I'm dying. Is this what dying feels like?*

As I came out of the fog, I realized where I was. A nurse came in to check on me. She said, "How are you feeling Miss Holly?" I explained, "I am in so much pain. Did something go wrong? Is this normal?" She told me, "We can give you some more pain medications. Everything went really well. This is normal. The pain just means your body is beginning to heal."

Within less than four hours of waking up, a physical therapist came into my room and said, "Miss Holly it's time to get you out of bed. I need to teach you how to get in and out of bed, how to get in and out of the car for when you go home, and the things you can and can't do for the next six months while your spine heals."

I looked at her and thought, *she's insane. There's no way I am moving or going anywhere. I am in way too much pain.* I asked her, "Do we have to start today? Can we wait until I feel better?" She replied, "No, we must get started today. The sooner we get you up and moving, the faster you will heal. I promise it will be painful now but it will provide relief much faster if we do this."

As I followed her instructions for getting out of bed, I felt as if the pain would make me pass out. The pain would swell to heights I didn't think I could possibly experience. I kept wondering, *is this normal? This can't be normal? Why did I even have this surgery? It hurts so much more. I can't possibly survive this.*

I was in the hospital for five days. During my stay the nurses came in and out of my room constantly. The physical therapist who I wanted to name "Torturer" forced me to do exercises every day. I dreaded the site of her. It meant I was about to experience alarming amounts of pain for the next hour. The pain was so bad all I could do was try to get through one minute, one surge of pain, one second more.

Even after going home, I had quite a few limitations for weeks and months. I couldn't lift anything heavier than a gallon of water for six months. I couldn't twist my spine or turn my neck for nine months while the fused bones calcified into their new position.

It took me a whole month to be able to manage by myself with day-to-day things like showering, dressing, walking the dog, making food, etc. And then, it took months to get slightly more active where I could walk longer distances.

Sadly, the pain continued for years. The surgery fixed the nerve pain, but then, I had a new problem—dealing with muscular pain from a spine that wouldn't move normally and the scar tissue from the surgery itself. There aren't many people who undergo such an extensive spinal fusion either.

When the surgeon finally visited me in my hospital room, he told me, "Holly the surgery went really well. I am confident you will live a full and normal life. There are a few limitations you will have for the next six months. And there are a few for life." Later I would find out that bungie jumping is a no. I also learned that sky diving was a no, but I did it twice anyhow and let them know it was fine. What the surgeon didn't tell me was that I would have to fight really hard to get and maintain a normal life with little to moderate pain.

Three years after that surgery I found myself addicted to muscle relaxants, consumed by my pain, and lost in suffering. A good friend of mine confronted me. Martina said, "It breaks my heart that you are in so much pain my dear friend. I love you and always will love you. You are forever my best friend. But I can't be your friend anymore. You are no longer the Holly I came to love and be best friends with. She is lost. You are so lost in your pain, you've lost yourself. I hope you find your way back. I am fighting for you and praying for you. But until you get back to being you, I can't be your friend. I'm so sorry."

At first, I was really angry with her. *Who is she to tell me that I can push through this? How can she possibly understand what I'm going through?*

And then I sat with what she said. I reflected on the previous few years and how bad they had been—how I was living a shell of my original self. The only thing I could talk about most of the time was my pain—how I was living off medications to get through each day. I had gained weight and lost my passion for exercise.

She was right. I had lost my identity. And so, I began my journey into recovery.

I slowly worked my way off the muscle relaxants. I found therapists, cognitive behavior experts, massage therapists, and other natural health pain experts to find a way forward without meds.

Honestly, the hardest part was the mental side. I had been consumed by so many negative thoughts about my body and my pain. I was living in a victim mindset—blaming others for my suffering, thinking, *why me.*

I was very angry with the world. Almost all my thoughts were about me and my pain. I didn't have room for anything else.

I started working on feeling my pain and imagining it releasing. I worked on my mindset. I worked toward believing there was nothing wrong with me or my body (that took years to believe). I worked on not speaking about my pain. I tried to listen to others. I began thinking about what else I wanted from life. I worked on being present.

One day I was having a drink with a good friend. She was sharing something important. Something very vulnerable. And my pain began to scream at me. But I knew I needed to be present for my friend. So I pushed my pain to the side. I said to my pain, *I hear you but my friend needs me. You aren't the center of my world anymore.* And I was able to stay present and listen to my friend. I'm so grateful I was able to. She was going through a difficult time. She needed someone truly listening to her so she knew she was important.

And yes, I would have moments when I would be present with my pain. The goal wasn't to ignore it, it was to learn how to have a relationship with it. One day I remember having a particularly bad day. Instead of pushing my pain away, I allowed myself to feel my pain. I sat with my pain. I breathed into it. I asked it, *what can I do to help you?* And I sat with it and listened. I asked my pain, *what are you trying to tell me or teach me?* And I sat once again with my pain and listened.

Not every time I do this do I get a clear message. But frequently I do. Sometimes it's that I need to take better care of myself. Sometimes it's that I need to be more flexible. Sometimes it's that I'm doing something to my body that I need to stop doing. But eventually it shares something I need to hear.

Another exercise I used frequently was imagining my pain was a tight fist. As the fist tightened, I would allow myself to fully feel the pain. Then I would slowly imagine the fist releasing its grip. And with it as I practiced this more, I could feel my pain let go, bit by bit.

Over time, as I worked with my health team, I slowly got better. The pain was no longer the center of my life. I found myself again. I began spending more time with family and friends. I started working out and set new goals. I began to believe I could live a normal life again.

The one thing that helped me the most was growing my spiritual life. At the time, I found a church I loved and began attending. I joined a small group and got involved with an amazing circle of women. That became my biggest support system for years. It helped me release my victim mindset. I finally felt supported. I felt safe. I felt loved.

A lot of our physical pain can reflect the emotional pain from our past manifested in our bodies. When we can't process or face what's happened to us emotionally, it will often show up in our bodies.

Louise Hay says that the back is about support—usually related to feeling unsupported by life. That absolutely described a lot of my suffering and pain from the past. I felt like I was adopted because I never fit in with my family. At school, I felt like an outcast or an alien. I felt like the weirdest person who didn't fit in anywhere. And so, I became isolated. I hid. So, of course, I didn't feel supported.

It took many years, and it still takes daily effort for me to maintain little to no pain, but it's possible. Now, I work with my physical therapist every three or four weeks and when I have a flair up. I work with my chiropractor every two to four weeks, my massage therapist once a month, and I have doctors I see quarterly as needed. I also work with a life coach and a spiritual-energy coach to keep my spirit and mind clean and clear, so I don't have new physical manifestations of suffering.

It took some time and work, but I was able to find my health care team. I was able to build the support I needed in life. And now, I live what I consider a better than average life. I am more fit, stronger, faster, and healthier than most people my age. I have energy and passion for my life. I can travel, have adventures, and pretty much do everything I want to.

If I can do this, you can too. It just takes you committing to the change and taking one small step each day. One step closer to freedom. One step closer to being pain-free. One step closer to building the life of your dreams with health at the foundation.

Are you inspired? Are you ready to build your health?

Great! You've got this! I'm with you every step of the way.

COMMIT TO THE JOURNEY

One really important part of the process is commitment. So, before we dive into the steps you'll need to optimize and boost your health, let's start by committing to the process.

Often, the process will have its speed bumps and setbacks. Accept this, expect it, and have ways to move forward regardless.

It may be helpful to have a friend, your spouse, or a colleague be your accountability partner throughout the process. Share with them what your goals are each day and week, and have them check in with you. Reach out to them when you get stuck and need help moving forward.

With any change we make, there is this process called letting go. We are letting go of parts of ourselves, things from the past, or habits we no longer want. Letting go can be a painful process, but it's also a freeing process. Be sure to take time to be gentle with yourself and take care of yourself. Consider doing something really nourishing for you each week.

In the chapter on self-care, we will talk about building your self-care menu. If you're concerned about needing a lot of support through this journey, you might consider starting with that chapter. Then, jump back into chapter three.

AN EXERCISE

Take out a piece of paper and write yourself a letter:

- Write today's date at the top.
- Write Dear [your name],
- Write what you're committed to changing in your life tied to your health.
- What are your goals?
- Where are you today with your health, and where do you want to be in 30-60-90 days from now?
- Write how you'll stay committed to the process (i.e., do you have an accountability partner, a coach, a mentor, or some way to check in?)
- Write a note of encouragement to yourself (i.e., You've got this, you can do this, etc.).
- Sign it.
- Put the letter in an envelope and put a date that's three months from today.
- Put it in a safe place where you can read it in three months.

Now you have committed to yourself, the most important person in your world, to change. To be better. To be the very best version of you. There's no turning back now. Don't let yourself down. Show up. You're worth it.

So, let's get started!

Change happens when you take action. Let's build your roadmap to health, vitality, and success.

If you want the companion course with all the materials referenced throughout this book (and more), please check out the health course here: https://hollyjeanjackson.com/healthsecrets

3

WITHOUT YOUR HEALTH, WHAT DO YOU HAVE?

"Habit is habit, and not to be thrown out of the window by any man, but coaxed downstairs a step at a time."

~ MARK TWAIN

Are you convinced that your health matters?

If not, let's start there. I want to explain why your health is the key to unlocking everything in your life and business.

When you aren't healthy, you can't show up at your best. You're likely tired, in pain, and distracted.

You can't focus on security—financial or otherwise. You won't be able to get clarity on what you desire. Figuring out what you're passionate about is impossible when you aren't healthy. Your passion is where you'll find your superhero skills—those skills and talents that only you can contribute to the world.

That is why getting to a place of health is key. We can't start living fully until we're healthy.

While writing this book, I found some daunting statistics. Less than 3% of Americans are living a healthy lifestyle. Overall, 71% of the adults surveyed did not smoke, 38% ate a healthy diet, 10% had a normal body fat percentage, and 46% got sufficient amounts of physical activity. (https://www.medicinenet.com/script/main/art.asp?articlekey=194453)

These statistics are scary. If we need a solid foundation, which includes our health, then we're falling short. We're failing as a country. We have gotten lost. We need to get back to the root of all healing—our lifestyle—making our health a top priority.

Too many of us rely on painkillers and quick fixes.

People go to the doctor expecting a prescription or easy solution to symptoms, but no one wants to do the work. No one wants to get to the root cause of what's going on. They want to mask their pain. Numb out. Not feel anything.

That is not living. That is the life of someone who has checked out—has given up. They're a shadow of a human. Ghosts perhaps.

Real health and healing start with lifestyle. Too many of my clients are unwilling to make the necessary changes because changing their lifestyles is challenging.

ANYTHING WORTH DOING IS DIFFICULT BUT ALSO EQUALLY REWARDING

Popping a pill or having surgery is not the whole solution. It may help mask the symptoms or fix your pain temporarily, but without taking a holistic approach, your pain will resurface.

There is no magic pill for good health. It takes dedication, lifestyle changes, and curiosity.

You must be curious about what is healthy for you. You're unique. You know what is best for your body, mind, and emotions. You must be your own advocate, exploring what works for you and your body.

No one diet or exercise routine works for everyone. It takes curiosity and willingness to experiment with new things to land on the right solutions. The right diet. The right exercise routine. The right self-care routine.

If you're already feeling overwhelmed, that's why I created a Health Secrets Master Class: https://hollyjeanjackson.com/healthsecrets To help you build a solid foundation with the tools you need to thrive—to help you discover what health means to you—to help you get more sleep, have more energy, reduce your pain, and so much more. This health course can be a companion to the book or a standalone resource to help you get healthier.

MY HEALTH ROLLER COASTER

I have personally lived, walked, stumbled, and suffered through my own battle with health.

I have battled chronic pain for most of my life. You read the story earlier. I had a spinal fusion in my early twenties that still gives me pain and requires incredible diligence and lifestyle shifts to manage.

I have endometriosis, an incredibly painful disease. I have had to find natural solutions to cope with my disease because my body cannot handle hormones.

I have healed from a severe concussion. Concussions are traumatic brain injuries and should never be taken lightly.

I have struggled with severe anxiety most of my life. It took decades, but I now know how to manage it.

Those are just some of the *big* health challenges. There are many others. There are many injuries, accidents, and emotional challenges I have faced over the years. And, of course, there's trauma. We all have it to various degrees. It requires healing just as much as our bodies need healing.

There are many different forms of health struggles. Those struggles are an invitation for us to grow. That calls us to get to an even better place.

If we're not facing challenges, how will we ever live our best life? How can we better support our bodies? How can we live without the pain that keeps us from living life full out?

Several years ago, I got the flu. Even though I was sick for less than a day, I ended up passing out on my way back to bed. I fell and landed on my face, damaging the frontal lobe of my brain.

I chipped three of my front teeth, needed stitches in my chin, had cuts on both of my arms, and black eyes from the impact of the fall.

Within the blink of an eye, my world turned upside down.

We walked into the emergency room and the nurses immediately rushed over to me. They saw the bruises on my face, bleeding from my chin, and the look of whiteness and shock in my face. They said, "What happened?"

"I passed out. I've had the flu and I got up to use the bathroom and I knew I was going to pass out but before I could get myself safely to the floor, I passed out from standing. When I woke up, I was bleeding, missing some teeth, and my right jaw and shoulder really hurt," I said.

They took me back to check my vitals and to run some tests including a CT scan. They pulled me aside and asked me, "Miss Jackson, did someone do this to you? Did your boyfriend beat you?" I answered, "No, of course not, but based on how little he seems to care tonight I can see why you might think he did."

They followed up, "Miss Jackson are you sure he didn't do this? We can keep you safe. We can call the police. You are safe." I reassured them, "He did not do this but I'm not sure he will be my boyfriend anymore. He seems more concerned about getting sleep than my health or pain."

They stitched up my chin. They gave me an IV for my dehydration, medications for the pain and sent me home. They advised me to follow up with my doctor and neurologist as soon as possible.

At first, I thought I got lucky. I did not have a lot of concussion symptoms for the first day or so.

Three days later, I began getting migraines, nausea and had extreme sensitivity to light and movement. I knew it was not normal.

I had had migraines in the past, but they were not severe and came infrequently. I scheduled an appointment with my neurologist. Based on my symptoms and her checkup, she shared with me that I had a *severe concussion.*

To allow my brain to heal to its full abilities, I read about all the natural ways I could improve my odds at having a normal life again.

It meant giving up alcohol and coffee for a year, eating healthy brain foods, and avoiding stress and anxiety. It also meant avoiding additional concussions for at least a year, if not forever. I didn't want to live in fear or stop living my life altogether.

I chose not to ride my bike for six months, and I was selective about risky activities to protect my brain. Injuring your brain back-to-back within a year will almost always cause irreversible damage. That was something I wanted to avoid. Riding my bike was simply not worth the risk.

I'll never forget taking Uber rides since I was not able to drive for months. My life was in the hands of those drivers. Way too many of them were terrible drivers. I was terrified I would get into a car accident and never be normal again.

I couldn't drive for six months. To this day, driving at night is overwhelming.

I was also terrified I would never be the same again. I felt like I would never be able to live a full life again.

A few weeks after my concussion, I went to play the piano. I have been playing for over twenty years. When I sat down to play a simple song, I couldn't do it without a getting a migraine. I had trouble concentrating. It was overwhelming. I couldn't do any work on the computer without headaches and confusion.

I could not handle being around large groups of people. I had to see people one-on-one for at least six months. I could not handle any daylight or bright lights for over a year. I still cannot handle music shows with a lot of bright lights. I have to wear special blackout glasses or close my eyes.

I also can't handle loud shows anymore and have to wear special earplugs, or I'll get a migraine. Concussions, mild or severe, are no laughing matter. Our brain is a big part of what makes us who we are. Without it, you can't get much done.

Honor your brain. Appreciate it. Keep it healthy.

In the first month of my recovery, I was laid off, which was ultimately a blessing. I was unable to work for the next seven months. I needed that time to recover and heal.

That gave me space to work on my stress and anxiety. I found a restorative yoga retreat in California and decided to attend. It was a five-day retreat in the woods. It was time to disconnect, meet other yogis, and work with my anxiety.

It was life changing. I had finally found my form of yoga. With my spinal fusion, most yoga classes cause me significant pain.

Gentle Therapeutics Yoga offered modifications using props that worked with all body types and injuries. It was amazing! I fell in love with yoga and meditation. It did wonders for my stress and anxiety levels.

For the first time, I was beginning to get a taste of what life in the present moment felt like. I remember one night we went into a restorative posture and did a meditation for an hour. I think this was the first time in my life where I was intentionally still.

As we went through this guided meditation, I could feel my body relaxing into the floor. I could feel the space between my thoughts for the first time ever. I could feel myself relaxing. I could feel my body and soul healing itself from within.

I felt safe. I felt supported. This was the first time I ever felt so calm, supported, and safe without being on medication. It felt so incredibly peaceful and free. I wanted to learn more. I knew I could never go back to the way life was.

From that experience, I ended up working with the teacher who ran the retreat to mentor me and teach me for my 200-hour teaching certificate. In that training, I dove even deeper into healing my anxiety, stress, sleep challenges, and physical health.

Yoga opened the door to healing my mind, body, and soul in a way that I never had access to before. It was a way of life I never knew existed.

The foundations of yoga are a way of living that helps you focus on the important things in life. I am so grateful for that experience. It was one of the most healing experiences in my life.

It would never have happened without my concussion. There is always a silver lining to every pain, injury, or event in our lives. We just have to be open-minded enough to see it.

In hindsight, I am grateful for my concussion. It was a wake-up call. Without it, I would never have had the time or challenges necessary to explore and fix my stress and anxiety. I would have continued doing life as-is. Just doing my best. Surviving, not thriving.

Often, when we're faced with a traumatic situation or health condition, it forces us to re-examine our lives. It reminds us just how precious and short life is. It shows us how fragile we are. How, in the blink of an eye, it could all disappear.

If you're in a challenging season and feeling helpless, I want you to know that you're not alone. There are millions of people in this country alone who are struggling with their health. We all have moments when we feel hopeless. We feel alone.

I'm here to tell you that you're not alone. Ever.

We all face challenging circumstances. We're all on a journey to either grow and improve or settle and suffer.

I'm here to show you the path forward for healing, growth, and transformation. For hope, joy, adventure, and fun.

Every day we choose to improve our health is a day we live life more fully. It gets us one percent closer to whole health and vitality.

The healthier we are, the more we can contribute to life, to those around us, and our loved ones. From excellent health stems energy, vitality, and creativity.

Without it, we experience depletion, depression, sadness, pain, and stuckness. We get backed into a corner when we're unhealthy. It limits our opportunities and options.

Choose to grow one percent healthier each day so that you crack open a door to endless possibilities.

You're worth it. Read on. Take action.

You've got this!

UNDERSTANDING YOUR PAIN

Many of our physical pains are manifestations of emotional hurts or things we have yet to process. It's our body's way of telling us that something is wrong. That we're unsafe. That we're unhappy. The list goes on. It can mean many different things.

As I dug deeper into my chronic migraines, I found that they were my body's way of telling me my life was out of alignment.

During one of my long-term relationships, my migraines continued to get worse for years, but when I left that relationship, they went away almost completely.

Another example of a flare-up was when I was traveling and not taking enough time to recover between trips or excursions. I would get more migraines. It was my body's way of telling me to slow down, to find more balance.

When we begin to shift our relationship to pain, it opens a new door. Instead of hating our pain, consider being curious about it. Build a relationship with it. Stop letting it drive everything in your life. Refuse to allow it to be the focal point of your life. But give it room to share. Listen to it. Let it tell you what's off kilter and show you where your life is out of balance. Magnify your blind spots.

When we tap into our bodies, magical things begin to happen. We can sense when people around us are bad for us or when loved ones are in pain and need our support. We can tell when we need to make more space for rest. We can sense if an opportunity is wrong for us.

We can begin to build a healthy life for ourselves when we tap in and tune in. But it takes courage, curiosity, and a relationship with our pain. And that can be scary.

MY PAIN IS ONE OF MY BIGGEST TRIGGERS.
AND YET, IT'S ALSO ONE OF MY MOST VALUABLE TOOLS
FOR LEARNING AND GROWING.

I love that song; *I Wish You Pain*, because it talks about how pain helps us grow. And there is wisdom and truth to that.

I don't wish anyone pain. But I do wish you growth from your pain.

Pain is part of being human. It's part of being alive. Pain allows us to grow. It allows us to be more sympathetic, compassionate, and relatable.

I believe my most painful experiences are what make me such a great coach and partner. I have a lot of depth and understanding of others' pain because I have personally walked that path. I understand. Not every circumstance, but I can relate in ways others cannot.

WHEN YOU CAN WALK THROUGH YOUR PAIN, YOU EXPERIENCE GREAT FREEDOM.

Notice I said "walk through" your pain, not avoid your pain. Not numb out your pain. Not mask your pain. I said when you face and walk through your pain, you'll gain freedom.

Facing our fears and pain provides us with great freedom and clarity. And great responsibility.

If you have been blessed with a life of pain, you have a responsibility to use it. Use it to help others. And yes, I said blessed. One of the first steps to navigating our pain is understanding we're not the victim.

We're not victims of our pain. Instead of asking why is this happening to me, ask why is this happening *for* me? What am I supposed to learn and gain from this experience?

I also want to note that I am still not perfect at this, far from it. There are times when a new health scare or pain season springs up, and I do not cope well with it. I start to spiral. I find myself triggered and going back into my victim mindset of *why me*.

But the key difference is, I don't allow this to happen for long. I have the tools to get out of the spiral.

I have a team of healers and health care providers to support me when I have a flare-up. I have coaches and mentors, and family to call me on my

BS. I have the system, tools, and people to navigate my pain and anything life throws my way.

And here's the good news.

YOU CAN DO THIS TOO!

You can have everything I just described. You simply start building it one piece at a time. This book has the tools and ideas to help you build the foundation you need.

Everyone's health foundation is unique. Each chapter will walk you through the pieces you can explore and experiment with to see exactly what you need to build into your life.

Now that we're clear on how important it is and how big of a gap there is for solid health in the world let's define what a solid health foundation means.

Please note: This will vary for each person. It is a framework of ideas to get your creative juices flowing.

YOU'RE YOUR OWN BEST DOCTOR AND HEALER

Use this framework and these tools as a starter kit for your health. Use the tools and experiment with what works best for you. Become an expert scientist and healer for your own body and life.

No one can tell you what works best for you. Only you know the answers to that. But it does take the willingness and curiosity to discover what exactly works for you.

We have a lot to cover. Let's dive in.

THE SOLID HEALTH FOUNDATION CHECKLIST:

If you have all of these in place, you have a solid foundation. However, there are ways to boost your health to the next level.

Read on to learn ninja skills to up-level your health foundation today.

As you continue through this book, I encourage you to build your personal health foundation checklist. It may have more or fewer items in it than listed here.

You're your own healer here. Take the reins. Be an experimenter and learn!

POSSIBLE HEALTH FOUNDATION CHECKLIST IDEAS:

Do You . . .

- get good sleep so you feel rested in the morning?
- have a daily routine?
- prevent pains that keep you from living your life and participating in activities you love?
- have the energy you need to accomplish your goals every day?
- wake up feeling excited to tackle the day (i.e., good sleep + mindset)?
- eat foods that give you energy?
- avoid foods that make you feel gross, bloated, or tired?
- stay at your ideal weight and feel great in your own body?
- have good thoughts about your life?
- avoid negative mental chatter (i.e., thoughts that bring you down)?
- have a positive outlook on life even when facing challenges?
- have a great support network and community?
- face and handle challenges without your entire world falling apart?
- have new goals to stretch into that next level of health (i.e., continuous improvement and student for life)?

How many of the items above were you able to say yes to? If it's less than ten, you have some work to do.

Regardless of where you are investing in your health, it is an investment in you, your life, and your future. It's always worth it. I promise you'll feel significantly better if you implement even just one thing from this book.

Taking even small actions for improvement can reap huge positive consequences. Imagine you improve your sleep, and that is all you work on. What would that open up for you in your life? In your business or work? In your spiritual life? In your travel, adventure bucket list?

I imagine that changing that *one* thing would open massive doors. It would be a *huge* needle mover. It would reap huge rewards.

I hope that makes you excited! I am truly excited for you! I can't wait to hear what works for you. But more importantly, I cannot wait to hear your stories—what transformations you experience—the meaning of those transformations in your life.

That is the whole reason I am writing this book. So you can find healing. So you can make an impact on this world.

WITHOUT YOU FIRST BEING HEALTHY, NO ONE ELSE WILL EVER EXPERIENCE THE SKILLS AND GIFTS THAT ONLY YOU POSSESS.

Are you still wondering if you have a solid health foundation?

The reality is this is an ongoing journey.

To truly optimize your health, you must continue to up-level it every day. Even if you're healthy today, there will still be nuggets of wisdom for you in this book. New ideas you'll want to try. New frameworks, tools, and processes to experiment with.

The idea here is to grow and get even healthier and to have fun while doing it!

One of the core tenets of good health is to reduce our stress levels. So, anything we can do to have fun, laugh and make our health a good experience is always a bonus.

I am here to walk you through this journey step by step.

4

SLEEP—
THE ROOT OF HEALTH

"The shorter you sleep, the shorter your life span."

~ MATTHEW WALKER, *WHY WE SLEEP*

I struggled with insomnia for years. Since I was a teenager, I got very little sleep. When I went to college, it worked to my benefit. I was taking extra classes each semester on top of working forty or more hours a week.

I would simply push through with little to no sleep each week and try to "catch up" on the weekends. Little did I know it was doing a lot of damage to my body and health. After college, my battle with insomnia continued.

It got to the point where I would go days without sleep. After three days of no sleep, I began to feel delusional. My hands were shaking. My eyelids wouldn't stop twitching. I felt like a zombie. The brain fog made it feel like I was sleepwalking through life. Everything felt challenging. Nothing was clear.

It felt like I was walking through quicksand with every move I made. Inside, I was terrified. *Is this going to kill me? Can you die from not sleeping? What am I going to do if I can't get sleep soon? I can't go on like this much longer. I feel like I'm losing my mind.*

When I saw my doctor about my insomnia, their solution was sleeping pills. They prescribed me Ambien. And after not sleeping for days, a pill that allowed me to sleep felt like a great solution . . . at the time.

For a long time, I continued using sleeping pills to break the insomnia cycles. Those pills are very addictive. They don't really fix the root cause of the problem. The side effects can also be quite debilitating.

I found myself relying on sleeping pills too often for "sleep." I put sleep in quotes because sleeping pills sedate you. They don't allow you to get real sleep or real rest. Sleep helps our bodies recalibrate, restore, and heal overnight. That's when we get real sleep.

I decided I needed to stop using Ambien after a few things happened. First, I learned of weird events that I couldn't remember. I would have an entire phone conversation or text chat that I didn't recall, but I would see or hear about it the next day. One night, I ate an entire jar of Nutella and couldn't recall doing it. I even drove somewhere one night, and when I woke up, I couldn't figure out how I had gotten there.

The final straw was when I took NyQuil and Ambien together one night because I was feeling sick. I woke up in the middle of the night to use the bathroom. When I got up to go back to bed, I passed out. My back crashed against the bathtub as I fell. My husband at the time found me on the bathroom floor convulsing and unconscious for several minutes.

The next morning, I went to the doctor to see what happened. He said, "Holly, you had what we call a vasovagal reaction. The Ambien prompted a stressor signaling your body to shut down to survive."

"You should no longer take Ambien. You need to be careful and stay hydrated for the next week. If you'd like, we can try prescribing you a different sleeping pill."

I said, "No. I need to find another safer solution to get sleep. One that won't do so much harm to my body."

I had bruises all over my back. I was achy and in pain for over a week.

What was even more challenging was getting past the addiction of using sleeping pills. I no longer had them as a crutch to lean on when I couldn't sleep for days. Not sleeping for days wasn't a solution either.

So, I got hyper-obsessed with sleep. So began my sleep journey.

I realized that a lot of my sleep problem was my anxiety. I had so much mental noise in my head when I would try to go to bed that it made it impossible to relax, much less sleep.

Here's an example of how it would go; I get into bed, I try to count sheep or breathe slowly. Then my mind was off to the races.

You forgot to put away that item. You might not remember to call your friend back. What if you miss that appointment tomorrow? What if you don't land that deal? What if my husband leaves me? What is wrong with me? Why is my pain level so high? Why do bad things keep happening to me? I wonder if Sally didn't like what I told her today. I still need to make plans for Saturday with Sophie. I'm not saving enough for retirement. I'll never be able to stop working. How did I get here? I'm a failure. I can't believe I put on five pounds this past year! I wonder how that happened. Am I lazy? Eating wrong? Is it just me? Am I destined to be fat?

You get the idea. My mind would spiral into what I forgot to do—where I might drop the ball—all the things I need to improve. I would wonder about all my biggest fears. I would wander down all these different choose your own journeys in one night, living and walking through each storyline as if it was really happening. It was exhausting.

I didn't seem to have any control over where my mind went. It was a jumble of fear, anxiety, and stress, along with my to-do list. And this would happen on repeat *Every. Single. Night.*

I'm sure many of you are nodding your heads in agreement. You've been there. Maybe you're there right now. You tried going to sleep. You failed. You decided to pick up this book and read about sleep because what you're doing is not working.

I worked on stress and anxiety tools that I could use throughout the day. That would help me manage my stress instead of waiting for it to build and unfold at nighttime before bed. I would do mini check-ins throughout the day with myself.

I began working with a behavioral therapist to get tools for how to break the cycle. It was a cycle I had been stuck in for over fifteen years. That's a *big* habit to break!

I saw a therapist to deal with the underlying stressors that I had been avoiding for years. I researched all the best sleep strategies and lifestyle changes I needed to make to get better sleep.

I won't lie. It took me years to break the cycle. But much of what I did in the first six months greatly improved my battle with insomnia. I stopped having such frequent bouts. When I do have them, I have tools to break the trend.

Now, I rarely have insomnia. If I do, it's usually from a medication I'm on temporarily, or it's my body telling me there's something I have not yet dealt with, and I need to heal.

Our bodies are incredibly wise. They're here to help us, guide us, and help us live our best lives. If you're experiencing insomnia or a lot of trouble with your sleep, you likely have some emotional things you have not dealt with. Your body is trying to tell you it's stuck in fight or flight mode—that something is wrong and that you need to fix it.

So, stop ignoring it. I urge you to use the tools and strategies I'm about to share so that you can rest and build a foundation where you can thrive.

I promise that if you implement these strategies and stick with them, within six to twelve months, you'll feel significantly better in every aspect of your life.

You'll have more mental clarity, more calm, more peace, more joy, less pain, and you'll be better equipped to handle stress. You'll have more energy.

And the best part is you'll know what you want out of life.

BECAUSE WHEN WE ARE EXHAUSTED OR IN PAIN,
NOTHING IS CLEAR.

When we remove those distractions and fix what ails us, we can open the door for so many possibilities!

WHY SLEEP?

Much of the content for why sleep comes from Matthew Walker's book, *Why We Sleep*. I'm summarizing and sharing some of the most compelling ideas from his book that have helped my clients and me.

One of the best ways we can optimize our health is to improve our sleep, get more of it, and make changes to our lifestyle to improve it.

Not convinced?

Here's the problem. We don't value sleep because scientists took so long to build the research behind its benefits. The data we now have is very convincing.

SLEEP IS THE FOUNDATION OF OUR HEALTH—WITHOUT IT, WE RUN INTO COUNTLESS HEALTH PROBLEMS

Our society has valued working long hours and being busy for far too long. It's not "cool" to value sleep. It's considered a sign of elevated status to work late and long hours.

The sad reality is that if you invest more time into getting quality sleep, you'll be much more productive at work with fewer hours. You'll also decrease the mortality and sick statistics in your workplace.

In this chapter, my goal is to explain the real science and data behind sleep—to prove that we are experiencing a sleep loss epidemic, convince you that sleep is the key to your health, and give you the strategies and tools to improve your sleep.

Perhaps you're thinking right now that you don't have a problem with sleep. If that is you, take the quiz below. On a sheet of paper, mark a checkbox for every Yes response.

SLEEP QUIZ FROM *WHY WE SLEEP*:

- After waking up in the morning, could you fall back asleep easily?
- Can you function without caffeine before lunch?
- If you didn't set an alarm clock, would you sleep past that time?
- Do you find yourself at your computer or desk reading and then rereading the same thing?
- Do you sometimes forget where you are while driving (i.e., you tune out)?

Okay now, don't cheat! Write the response to your answers to the above questions before reading this paragraph.

If you responded Yes to any of the questions above, you still have room to improve your sleep.

Even if you responded No to all the questions above, I urge you to read this chapter. There is always room for improvement in every aspect of our lives. Sleep is *way* too important to skip over.

For those of you who are analytical and need the facts, I have pulled a few of the most powerful statistics together that I have found in my reading and research. These are the numbers I share when I speak or present on sleep and energy.

SLEEP FACTS:

- The World Health Organization has now declared a sleep loss epidemic throughout industrialized nations.
- One person dies in the US due to a fatigue-related error each hour. (Sleepless in America, National Geographic)
- Every single organ and process of the body positively benefits from sleep and is detrimentally impaired by not getting enough. (Sleepless in America, National Geographic)

"Routinely sleeping less than six or seven hours a night demolishes your immune system, more than doubling your risk of cancer."

~ MATTHEW WALKER

As you can see, we have a *big* sleep problem. And it's only getting worse. In fact, as I write this book, we are over a year and a half into the COVID-19 pandemic. Researchers have shown the statistics on higher suicide rates, domestic violence, anxiety, health challenges are on the rise, and much more.

Additionally, we are seeing signs of increasing numbers of insomnia. Pandemics bring out a lot of fear for people. Fear and anxiety are the enemies of quality sleep. They trigger insomnia. We have a massive sleep problem on our hands, and it's only getting worse.

So, why are we talking about this first in terms of your health?

Here are some of the benefits of good sleep.

BENEFITS OF QUALITY SLEEP:

- Sleep enriches a diversity of functions: the ability to learn, memorize, and make logical decisions.
- Sleep recalibrates our emotional brain circuits.
- Sleep restocks the armory of our immune system.
- Sleep regulates our appetite.
- Dreaming mollifies painful memories, increases creativity, and much more.
- Sleep maintains a flourishing microbiome within your gut.
- Sleep lowers blood pressure while keeping our hearts in fine condition.
- The physical and mental impairments caused by one night of bad sleep dwarf those caused by an equivalent absence of food or exercise.

So how did we get here?

CHALLENGES TO PRIORITIZING SLEEP

The biggest challenge we face in fixing our sleep deprivation epidemic is that we don't value sleep. Our society has built systems, companies, school systems, and schedules that don't work for different sleep profiles.

Not everyone is meant to be an early riser. Not everyone is a night owl. And yet, our systems and companies have designed everything around the early riser. If we designed school systems around providing the best experience for our children while optimizing their health, we would open schools later in the day.

Children need even more sleep than adults because they're developing and that only becomes more important as they hit adolescence. Schools should open in the late morning or early afternoon. That way, students will get the sleep they need, perform better, and would likely result in better test results.

Before the pandemic, companies have forced adults to juggle crazy commute times, long work hours, and global schedules that make prioritizing sleep nearly impossible. How can we get good sleep when our society doesn't value it?

The COVID-19 pandemic has provided us with an opportunity to re-evaluate work environments. We can also set better boundaries with our employer, ask for schedules that suit us with solid arguments based on data, and negotiate for what we need to thrive at work and home.

We are in this epidemic because there wasn't science to prove how vital sleep is until quite recently.

Another challenge we face is our overuse of caffeine. Caffeine is the most widely used and abused psychoactive stimulant in the world.

Most of us don't fully understand how much caffeine impacts our sleep. Caffeine blocks the sleepiness signal normally communicated to the brain by adenosine, giving you a false sense of wakefulness.

Caffeine has an average half-life of five to seven hours. That means that if you have a cup of coffee at 3:00 p.m., only half of it has been processed through your system by 8:00 to 11:00 p.m. That will impact your body's ability to feel sleepy and fall asleep at a reasonable hour.

One cup of decaf usually contains 15-30% of the dose of a regular cup of coffee. Some people are sensitive to caffeine and are not able to break it down very quickly. As we age, it takes our brain and body even longer to remove caffeine from our system. As we age, we should consume less coffee.

If you're struggling with sleep, one of the first things you might consider is giving up caffeine. Or, at the very least, reduce how much caffeine you consume. Try to avoid caffeine after 1:00 p.m. That alone may move the needle enough to improve your sleep *a lot*.

Another massive challenge we face in our sleep problem is the use of sleep supplements. That includes natural sleep supplements.

There are no past or current sleeping medications on the legal or illegal market that can induce natural sleep, and natural sleep is our goal. If we want the benefits of sleep, we must make lifestyle changes to obtain real sleep.

Most sleeping pills induce what's called rebound insomnia. You take them, and you're able to get a night or two of good "sleep." But once you stop taking them, you have insomnia for a night or two.

That makes sleeping pills incredibly addictive. It also fools us into thinking we are getting sleep. Sleeping pills are sedating our bodies. They're not actually inducing real sleep.

Studies have also found that drugs like Ambien cause memory loss. Countless researchers have found that people taking sleeping pills are 4.6 times more likely to die over 2.5-years compared to those who are not using them. Even people who use sleeping pills occasionally (eighteen times or less within a year) are 3.6 times more likely to die than those who do not use them at all.

Given the mortality statistics, it's shocking that sleeping pills are still prescribed without careful oversight. Sleeping pills are so addictive and have so many negative consequences; I believe they should be more carefully regulated.

There are situations where we need sleeping pills to break a cycle of insomnia that natural solutions can't. However, they should be carefully managed. They should not be the only solution to getting sleep and combating insomnia.

Even using natural supplements like Melatonin can have negative consequences. When people overuse natural supplements like these, it inhibits our body's ability to produce hormones naturally. Many of these natural hormones in our body regulate when we feel tired. If we overuse them, it throws our system off. Eventually, we won't be able to produce them at all, and we will be reliant on taking supplements.

We should do our best to make changes to our lifestyle that improve our sleep versus using medications.

We should obsess over the science behind sleep. We should be empowered to experiment with ways to improve our sleep through strategies that work naturally.

BECAUSE SLEEP IS THE KEY TO EVERYTHING

Science shows that the gut is the highway to good health. But without sleep, your body can't reset and heal overnight. The gut won't function at its optimum levels without natural sleep.

Have you noticed that everything seems easier and better after a good night's sleep? It's because it *is* better. When we sleep, we are able to process emotional challenges and come up with solutions to things we couldn't solve the day before. We wake up feeling better, which frees us up to handle stressful situations.

The old saying, "Let's sleep on it," is great wisdom. A good night's sleep is often what we need to solve problems, cure what ails us, and much more.

So hopefully, now you're convinced. You see the problem we face and how we got here. Now, how do you fix it in healthy ways that will provide you with real quality sleep?

I have several strategies for you to consider. Let's dive in.

SLEEP STRATEGIES

Here are several strategies that will help you improve your sleep. The more you implement them, the better your quality and quantity of sleep will be. Visit this link to get a copy of the Sleep Strategy Worksheet for reference: https://coachhollyjackson.activehosted.com/f/37

STRATEGY ONE: STICK TO A SLEEP SCHEDULE

If you have work schedule flexibility, become a scientist about your sleep schedule. Get curious about the best time of the day for you to wake up. If you didn't set an alarm, what time would you naturally wake up? At the end of the day, when are you naturally sleepy?

Once you discover your natural circadian rhythm (when your body naturally feels sleepy and awake), make a conscious effort to stick to it. Having a regular time to go to bed and wake up will help your brain and body's natural circadian rhythm release the proper hormones for sleep at the right time.

If you don't have a flexible work schedule and must get up at a specific time, do the math and subtract eight hours from your wake-up time. That should give you your ideal bedtime. It takes most of us ten to thirty minutes to fall asleep. Additionally, science shows that getting at least seven hours of sleep each night is optimal for healing and recovery.

Even on the weekends, do your best to stick to your schedule. It makes a huge difference.

When traveling, be gentle with yourself. It takes one day per time zone crossed for your circadian rhythm to adjust. Give yourself ample time to adjust and recover upon returning home.

STRATEGY TWO: THINGS TO AVOID

Several things that could be impeding your ability to get rest. Some may even seem like healthy things to do. Here are some things you should avoid if you're having trouble getting quality sleep.

Exercise is great for helping you sleep. However, if you exercise too close to bedtime, it actually wakes up your body. It makes it impossible to fall asleep on time.

Be sure to avoid exercising two to three hours before bedtime. Play around with what time of day is best for your body—where you reach peak performance and can still fall asleep according to your optimal sleep schedule.

Avoid caffeine, nicotine, and alcoholic drinks before bed. And if you're really struggling with sleep and, in particular, insomnia, remove them from your diet altogether. It could be a game-changer for your sleep. Alcohol is a depressant and sedates the body. While it may help some people fall asleep, many find themselves waking up in the middle of the night or sleeping restlessly when drinking.

In the challenges section, we already discussed caffeine and how it impacts our body's ability to release the hormones that make it feel sleepy and ready to go to bed. Avoid drinking caffeine after 1:00 p.m. for optimal sleep.

Marijuana also negatively impacts our sleep. It doesn't allow us to get as much deep or REM sleep. If you're feeling tired after a night of sleep, consider removing marijuana from your routine.

You'll also want to avoid large meals and beverages late at night. Eating a large meal right before bed can create indigestion, making sleep difficult. It also forces your body to spend a lot of energy digesting your food, which can inhibit its release of natural sleep hormones. Going to sleep right after a large meal can create heartburn or gas as well, making deep rest impossible.

Having beverages close to bedtime will make it difficult to remain asleep for the duration of the night. If you struggle with staying asleep, consider limiting your fluid intake as you get close to bedtime, especially teas, even if they're caffeine-free as they're diuretics and will make you urinate more frequently.

While naps can be healthy, there are do's and don'ts regarding naps and your sleep routine. When napping, make sure you don't nap after 3:00 p.m. When napping during the day, set an alarm for twenty minutes. That's plenty of time for an optimal nap that will not throw off your circadian rhythm—napping too long or after 3:00 p.m. will throw off your natural sleep rhythm. We want to optimize our body's ability to do what it does best—sleep and heal.

And the last big no-no is that if you can't fall asleep, do *not* remain in bed. Get out of bed. Do something restful until you feel sleepy. Then try to go back to bed. You should not stay in bed for more than twenty minutes awake. Your bed should only be used for sleeping and intimacy. Not for anything else, especially if you struggle with sleep or insomnia.

STRATEGY THREE: SLEEP HYGIENE AND YOUR SLEEP OASIS

Strategy two had some items that bleed into our sleep hygiene, but here are a few more pointers.

I want you to create a sleep sanctuary that works for you. Experiment with what you need in your bedroom to help you fall asleep fast and stay asleep.

Create a dark, cool, and quiet space to sleep in. Consider removing any technology or light sources from the bedroom. Purchase blackout curtains to keep out daylight. Play with different smells. Some people like using a diffuser and having lavender in their room to induce rest, relaxation, and sleep. After using certain scents for a time, it will trigger a natural response from your body to rest and sleep. The ultimate goal is to create the perfect oasis for you to sleep and restore.

Make sure your mattress is the right one for how you sleep. If you're a side sleeper or have a tight low back, consider purchasing a softer mattress with memory foam. If you're a back sleeper, consider a firm mattress.

Remove sleep distractions as much as possible. If you're a light sleeper, consider purchasing a noise machine or earplugs. Consider wearing an eye mask if you can't remove all forms of light in your bedroom.

STRATEGY FOUR: BEDTIME ROUTINES THAT WORK

Once you build your sleep oasis, you need to dial in your bedtime routine. That's right. Even though you're an adult now, you too need a bedtime routine. You can download a copy of My Bedtime Routine worksheet here for other ideas: https://coachhollyjackson.activehosted.com/f/32

Ideally, an hour before bedtime, you want to create a ritual that will help you go from the day's activities to restful sleep. It's your segue into a peaceful night of sleep.

SOME IDEAS TO CONSIDER FOR YOUR BEDTIME ROUTINE:

- Take a hot bath before bedtime. That will help your body temperature drop, and you'll fall asleep more easily.

- Turn off bright lights and use rock salt lamps or dim candles before bed. Bright lights don't allow the body to release Melatonin, which tells us we are tired.

- Do something relaxing. Read a book. Do some gentle yoga, meditation, or journaling. Experiment with a relaxing activity that helps calm the mind and move into relaxation.

- Reflect on the day with your partner. Say one thing you accomplished that day, one thing you need to work on, and one thing you're grateful for. That will help you reflect, unwind, and connect. It will also bring you closer together.

Get curious about what helps you relax the most, and do that every night before bedtime. It will make a tremendous difference in your quality and quantity of sleep.

SLEEP STRATEGY FIVE: EXPERIMENT WITH YOGA NIDRA

Yoga nidra is a yogic state of sleep. It's an easy and safe form of sleep and rest. Many people use it as a tool to fall asleep. They add it to their bedtime routine, especially when they're stressed or in pain. It allows them to move into a natural state of sleep gently and easily.

BENEFITS OF YOGA NIDRA:

- Helps put your brain into a state of theta waves, similar to sleep, allowing your organs and systems to reset
- Helps eliminate anxiety, depression, stress and increases overall wellbeing
- A single session can increase dopamine levels by 65%
- Anyone can do it anywhere, and it's easy to do!
- It offers an opportunity for you to get to know yourself more deeply
- Combats PTSD symptoms
- Fights insomnia

To give yoga nidra a try, all you need to do is Google yoga nidra. There are many guided YouTube resources and other tools available.

It's a wonderful tool to use if you're struggling with insomnia. It's also great for new moms who can't get long chunks of sleep.

One hour of yoga nidra is said to have the benefits of four hours of natural sleep. It's a great way to catch up on natural rest and healing when you can't get seven hours of sleep. It's *not* meant to be a replacement, though.

Another sleep recording I like to use when my insomnia is really bad or even when I'm traveling is Kelly Howell's *Universal Mind Meditation*. The recording uses theta waves to help your brain relax and get your body into a state of deep wakeful rest.

It usually helps me fall asleep even when I'm ultra-stressed or in pain. Even if I'm unable to fall asleep, I'm still getting a similar form of rest to that of yoga nidra when I'm still and listening. Be sure to listen to this recording with earbuds to get the most out of it, as the theta waves are specific to each ear and side of the brain.

Utilize all these sleep strategies, and I guarantee you'll greatly improve your sleep, healing, and recovery. Your body, mind, and soul will thank you.

Want to give yoga nidra a try?

Get a copy of my yoga nidra recording here: https://coachhollyjackson.activehosted.com/f/39

5

SELF CARE ISN'T SELFISH

"If you don't love yourself, nobody will.
Not only that, you won't be good at loving anyone else.
Loving starts with the self."

~ WAYNE DYER

Another thing our society doesn't value enough is self-care. Instead, we are high-fived for working crazy hours, getting little sleep, pulling all-nighters, and burning the candle at both ends.

And we wonder why we have so many health challenges. When we don't take care of ourselves, of course, we will get sick. We have more pain. We have more diseases.

Most of us learn this lesson the hard way. We try to push through the pain. We pop pills. We get injections to numb the pain. We ask our doctor for the next thing that will get us back on our feet the fastest. We opt for surgeries to solve issues that we could fix ourselves.

The list goes on and on . . .

Our society values productivity. We value hard work. We do not value our health.

As I write this, we are in the middle of a pandemic. And while this is helping us value health more, I'm not convinced it's turned things around enough.

We have an uphill battle.

> ## UNTIL WE EACH ACCEPT THAT HEALING IS AN INSIDE JOB, WE CAN'T CHANGE ANYTHING.

It's our responsibility to fix our health. To advocate for ourselves. To make the necessary changes in our lifestyles to thrive.

SO, WHAT IS SELF-CARE?

Self-care is the individual practice of health management without the aid of a medical professional. In health care, self-care is any human regulatory function under individual control, deliberate and self-initiated, to maintain health and wellbeing.

Self-care is empowering. The very definition shows that it's up to the individual to manage their health without a medical professional. You may get ideas from a professional, but it's up to you to do the work.

For example, a physical therapist can give you exercises to do at home. Self-care is the act of performing those exercises routinely.

If you take nothing away from this chapter, please take this to heart.

> ## SELF-CARE IS *YOUR* RESPONSIBILITY. YOUR HEALTH IS ONE HUNDRED PERCENT UP TO YOU.

MY JOURNEY WITH SELF-CARE

I can speak to this because I used to fall victim to it. I used to blame others, God, the world, karma, you name it, for my pain and suffering. I kept repeating the same insane pattern for years, denying that I had any power to change things.

I would suffer from some major life challenge, and it would be coupled with a new health diagnosis. And I would just think, *why me? Why does this keep happening to me? Why am I so unlucky? What's wrong with me?*

Instead, I should have been asking, *what do I need to change in my life to fix this pattern?* When we ask "why," it's disempowering. There are no good answers and certainly no solutions.

WHEN WE ASK "HOW," IT OPENS THE DOOR TO POSSIBILITY, CREATIVITY, AND SOLUTIONS.

The more we can get curious, the more we can find solutions. The more empowered we are, the better equipped we are to take action that will help us.

Don't make the same mistake I did. Stop blaming. Accept responsibility for your situation. Get curious. Start asking what you can change in your life and how. Remove the "why" question from your thinking altogether.

When I went through my divorce, I fell deep into the victim trap. And that had been going on for years leading to the divorce. I was in a verbally abusive relationship. My husband would call me names. He would say terrible things to me, like, "You being born is what drove your dad to become an alcoholic."

He would say endearing things followed very quickly by a horrible, demeaning comment like, "You'll never do anything meaningful. You're horrible at communication. You'll never have real friends."

After hearing comments like that from the person you commit your life to, the person who is supposed to love you, it breaks you. Slowly, over time, you lose your identity. You allow them to start painting the picture of who you are.

I remember thinking, *Holly, you're such a failure. You need to stay in this marriage because it's the best you deserve. You really are terrible at communicating. No one wants to be your friend. You're ugly, fat, hideous. No one will ever want you. He's right. You need to do better.*

When he told me he wanted a divorce, I fought to keep the marriage going. That's how lost I was. Then one day, he did something truly awful. We went to counseling. Things seemed to be improving. He said, "I would like to make love. Are you ready for that?" I said, "Only if you're 100% committed to making this work. Only if you aren't going to just turn your back on me." He said, "Of course not, I would never do that. I'm in this." And so, we were intimate.

After that, he went on a four-day work trip and never called or even texted. He did exactly what I asked him not to do. And he knew that it would hurt me deeply. When he returned, I asked, "Why did you do that? You knew that would hurt me?" His response was, "Oh baby, you know you wanted it." At that point, I lost it. I was officially done. I never turned back from that moment on. I told him, "Get out of my house. Get out of my life. We are done. I never want to speak to you again. It's over!"

That was a turning point for me. That situation forced me out of victim mode. I was finally out of his grip. He no longer had control over me.

Once I was finally awake, I realized how much I had lost. I lost my identity. I had become a shell of who I was. Slowly, over time, he had managed to control me. He had changed my perspective about who I was as a person. I believed his every word.

Once I snapped out of it, I was furious, but also relieved. Grateful to be me again. Ready to start rebuilding. I promised myself from that moment on; I would never allow anyone to do that to me again. I would never compromise so much of myself that I would lose myself completely. I would never allow anyone to treat me that way again.

I also decided to get help. I joined Celebrate Recovery, to work on my codependency issues—to take back what was mine in that situation—to make sure it never happened again.

You see, there are many ways we can lose ourselves. Many ways that our life or bodies tell us we need more self-care.

My divorce was one of the most extreme experiences that showed me how much I needed to take better care of myself—especially my mental and spiritual health.

At first, it felt overwhelming. It felt impossible.

I had relied on my husband for such a long time to take care of everything. I had forgotten how driven, capable, strong, fierce, and able I was . . . and am. Once I started taking small steps forward, I felt so strong and empowered.

As I navigated my divorce, there were a lot of things I had to do. I had to find a new job, a new place to live, a church to join to start building connections and support, get new health insurance . . . the list was long.

I put my project manager hat on. I got into action. And with each action, I felt better.

I'll never forget that first day I moved into my apartment alone. I felt so much freedom and relief. It was the first time in a long time that the only living being I needed to take care of was myself.

I actually had the space and capacity to take care of me. I was no longer burdened by making meals for someone else, cleaning, and doing things for my husband.

It made tuning into my needs so much easier. Because I had a lot of anger and emotion to process, I started running. I joined a running group. I ran so many miles for that first year. I don't think I would have survived without it.

I would go on runs and cry. I would run and scream on the inside. Running was my therapy to process all the hurt and suffering from an abusive relationship.

I started working with a therapist. I made new friends and new plans with old friends. I made plans to travel. I worked on fixing my finances. I reconnected with my family.

I even created a Friday night ritual of dating myself. I would try a new fancy recipe, buy a nice bottle of wine, or rent a movie I wanted to watch. And I would date myself.

My goal was to fall in love with myself. I didn't want to date anyone until I was 100% in love with all of me. I didn't want to repeat an abusive relationship. I wanted to be the best version of me before dating.

I went on all the hikes, backpacking trips, and adventures I couldn't go on while I was married. I did all the things my husband told me I couldn't.

In some ways, it felt like I was a recovering cancer patient. I was given a new lot in life. I could do life however I wanted. I got my time back. I got my happiness, peace, and freedom back.

I felt like I could do anything. I felt more alive than ever. Ready to take on life.

That season of empowerment, peace, and happiness went on for a while. But then, a couple of years down the road, I discovered I had not fully broken the pattern. I had another layoff and health challenge.

Initially, I went into victim mode. But I knew better and broke that cycle quickly. I hate to say that this cyclical lesson for me is an ongoing lesson. I get better over time, but I haven't fully broken it.

My friends call me Jetpack because I like to move fast. Because I have a thirst for life. Because I'll take *big* goals on. And that is great. It's a big part of who I am.

But it's also what gets me into trouble. I take on too much. I push myself too hard and forget about taking care of me. I frequently don't realize how much stress I'm under until a friend or my partner points it out to me. I get into the jetpack zone, but I take it too far.

What I have discovered is that it's an ongoing juggling act. I can't say it's a balance because it's changing too often to truly call it that. But I can say that when I have a lot of new pain or a situation that throws me off, it's a signal that my life is out of sorts—that I'm out of flow—off the path.

And now that I know the signals, it's easier to course-correct.

When I get frequent migraines, it's usually because something in my love life is off or I'm pushing myself too hard.

When I get a lot of neck or back pain, it's because I'm stressing and not allowing myself enough downtime for relaxation, or my mental thinking is way off.

When I have insomnia, it's because my thinking is *way* off. When my anxiety flares up, it's because I need to take more time to do meditation and yoga. Or it's because I haven't processed something emotionally.

Now, I'm in tune with my body and its signals. I know what it's telling me. And when I can't figure it out, I have a team that can help me.

I'm better equipped to prepare for when I need to boost my self-care. For me, I need a lot of self-care when I have a new health challenge. My health is my biggest trigger.

I also need a lot of self-care when I'm traveling. My body needs a lot of nourishment when moving across time zones and experiencing a lot of change.

When I'm making big life changes, I need more self-care. For example, when I'm moving to a new city, a new job, or starting a new endeavor in my business. Those are signals that I need to take more time to sleep, restore, and reflect.

I need to check in and listen to my body to thrive in life and to reduce new health problems. Most of my health challenges come from trying to push through without self-care.

I USED TO THINK THAT SELF-CARE WAS NAUGHTY.
THAT IT WAS LAZY. THAT IT WAS FOR THE WEAK. NOW,
I REALIZE THAT SELF-CARE IS FOR THE STRONG, WISE,
GENEROUS, AND THOSE WHO WANT TO *WIN BIG* IN LIFE.

If we can't take care of ourselves, we have nothing to offer those around us.

I still have occasional guilt when I take a lazy day but not nearly as much as I used to. In fact, now I celebrate taking care of myself even when I'm unable to check everything off my to-do list. I celebrate making myself my top priority.

I can't accomplish anything without my health, and neither can you.

THE DAUNTING REALITY WE FACE

We are facing a stress and anxiety epidemic. And it's global.

While 33% of people report feeling extreme stress, *77% of people experience stress that affects their physical health*. And 73% have stress that impacts their mental health. Another 48% have trouble sleeping due to stress. The statistics are even more extreme for women and single parents. (https://www.therecoveryvillage.com/mental-health/stress/related/stress-statistics/)

Stress is related to some pretty significant health issues: heart disease, high blood pressure, diabetes, depression, and anxiety. Those add significant costs to our healthcare system. They create absences in the workplace and stressors on families. The impact is huge.

STRESS IS NOT GOING AWAY

The things that cause us stress are here to stay. Money, relationships, work, the economy, family responsibilities, personal health issues, job stability, personal safety, moving, and grieving the loss of a loved one.

It's part of being human. So, we need to find better ways to cope. Better ways to take care of ourselves. To manage our stress and anxiety.

Given that stress has that much of a negative impact on our mental and physical health, we must take better care of ourselves. We must make self-care a priority.

BUILDING YOUR PERSONAL SELF-CARE MENU (I.E., YOUR LIFE RAFT!)

Still not convinced that taking care of you is worth your time? I get it. I've been there.

I've been in seasons of life when I just pushed through. I needed to simply survive. But the reality is that even those situations would have been easier to navigate if I hadn't stopped taking care of myself.

As we explore the benefits of self-care please take notes on which ones resonate most with you—which ones you're most open to or excited to try. This section will help you to get started on building your own personal self-care menu.

Visit this link to get Your Self-Care Worksheet: https://coachhollyjackson.activehosted.com/f/30 Use this tool to build your menu today.

This tool will serve you well. It's something you can look at when you're having a bad day, faced with a big challenge, are in incredible pain, are really sick, or when you're sad or deeply depressed.

This menu will serve as your compass to healing—your personal guide to getting back on track and back to thriving in life. This menu is your lifesaver when you feel you're floating out to sea—pulled away by the challenges of life.

So, let's explore some of the benefits of self-care so you can start building your lifesaver today.

BENEFIT 1–YOU'LL SLEEP BETTER

When you take good care of yourself, it helps balance your mental health. When we don't stop to take care of ourselves, our mental health suffers rapidly.

In our previous chapter, we discussed the importance of having good sleep hygiene, a solid bedtime routine, and much more. Sleep and self-care go hand in hand.

- *Implement good sleep strategies.* Getting good sleep is part of good self-care. And implementing strategies like good sleep hygiene, bedtime practices to help you fall asleep, and finding the best time of day to work out without impacting your sleep routine is all part of good self-care.

- *Take time to unplug.* When you stop to take a breather, take a walk in nature, read a book for fun, or go for a pedicure with a girlfriend, it always improves your outlook on life. And it will make it much easier to fall asleep because you'll find yourself in a much happier and peaceful state.

- *Make your self-care a priority.* Everything is easier and clearer when you take good care of yourself. If your self-care routine is dialed in, when your head hits the pillow, it should be easy to fall asleep. And when you're having trouble falling asleep and find your mind spinning, it means your self-care needs some attention.

BENEFIT 2-YOU'LL STRENGTHEN YOUR IMMUNE SYSTEM

The science behind our immune system and health has shown that self-care, and thus our lifestyle, is at the heart of a solid foundation for health. If you're socially disconnected, disengaged, not exercising, not getting good sleep, etc., it's likely that your health will suffer.

- *At the heart of being a happy human is connection—community.* So, if you've been feeling depressed, ill, or having more pain, consider this. Try connecting with a friend for coffee. Find a group to join and get involved. Find ways to connect with others, to engage in your community. You'll feel happier, and your health will thank you.

- *Perform an act of kindness.* When we do something nice for others, it makes us feel good. We feel connected, purposeful, valued, and happy.

  If you're feeling off or down, consider doing a small act of kindness for someone you care about or even a complete stranger. And then, reflect on how it feels to share kindness. Add that to your self-care menu if you like how it feels. Come back to it as a tool when you're feeling off.

- *Go outside every day.* Research has shown that spending time outside lowers your stress levels, boosts your immune system, and lowers your blood pressure. And self-care, like making time to regularly go outside, helps you get better sleep, completing the circle. Making self-care a priority can also reduce your risk of developing heart disease and type II diabetes. All it takes is just a few minutes a day. Go outside for a three to five-minute walk every day.

- *Exercise daily.* Part of excellent self-care is taking care of your body. That means moving every single day. Exercise helps boost your immune system and manage your stress levels while stabilizing your mood. Daily movement helps your mental and physical wellness in numerous ways. All it takes is twenty to thirty minutes of activity a day.

BENEFIT 3-YOUR RELATIONSHIPS WILL IMPROVE

When we make self-care a priority, our relationships will naturally improve. When we take care of ourselves, we can show up as the best versions of ourselves. That means we can be better parents, friends, employees, and members of our communities. There are many elements of self-care that allow more space for relationships. Here are a few:

- *Prioritize your to-do list.* When you're clear on your life priorities and career or business goals, it's easy to prioritize your to-do list. At times, our to-do lists grow quite long. It can be very overwhelming. Sometimes our lists can even paralyze us. They're so big; we don't even know where to start.

  Knowing your values and life priorities will give you clarity. That will give you peace of mind. And at the end of the day, you'll feel more accomplished. You'll have achieved what was most important on your list while still having time to spend with loved ones.

- *Learn to say no.* Part of prioritization is being clear on what you need to say *no* to. If it's not on your priority or values list, it's a no. You can say no politely, but it's still a no. People make the mistake of saying yes to others. They want to please them. But it comes at great sacrifice.

  When we say yes to things that aren't important to us, it forces us to say no to things that will help us hit our goals. It closes the door on critical opportunities. We feel like we are missing out when our priorities are out of whack or undefined.

- *Define success for yourself.* What does this have to do with self-care? If you don't know what you want from life, you'll ultimately say yes to things that others want from you. You'll run in circles getting burnt out. You'll feel unhappy—possibly bitter.

  When you define success on your own terms, you're empowered to say yes to what's right for you—to say no to what's not. You'll no longer be a victim of life. You can sail your own ship when you know where you want to go.

  Do *not* wait to do this. It takes time and reflection, but it's critical to your happiness, health, and wellbeing.

- *Let yourself relax and have fun.* When we are children, we understand how to play, how to have fun, and how to relax. As adults, we often forget how to do it. Allow yourself space and time to relax. To have fun. To play. To be creative. To let your inner child thrive!

BENEFIT 4—BETTER FINANCES!

When you're clear on your values and priorities, it makes building your financial future much easier. You have clear goals. I can't tell you how many people I know who are unhappy and they take it out on their wallets. They think they can buy happiness. They go on shopping binge sprees only to discover that they still have a hole in their life.

When we don't take care of ourselves, it leads to addiction. Whether that's sex addiction, alcoholism, food addiction, or shopping. Regardless of the addiction, it will take its toll on your health, life, and your wallet.

To have a healthy financial picture, you must make self-care a priority. When you are happy and healthy, it's much easier to set and follow a budget—to build healthy and reasonable financial goals. To be successful on our own terms.

So, let's dig into your self-care menu options for your financial wellbeing.

BUILD OUT YOUR FINANCIAL GOALS.

Map out your goals over the next one, five, ten, and fifteen years from today.

Feeling stuck?

Here are some ideas for you to consider:

- **Debt:** If you have credit card debt, when would you like to have that paid off? And how will you go about making that happen? What other debt do you have? How will you pay that off?

- **College Savings:** If you're a parent, what are your goals for a college savings account? If your child is going to college in ten years, what's your payment plan to save enough to help them?

- **Home Ownership:** Looking to buy a house? How long will it take you to save enough for a down payment? What mortgage amount can you afford? What's your plan to make it happen?

- **Retirement:** How does your retirement account look? Do you have a 401k? Are you contributing enough for your retirement goals? Do you have a rollover IRA or Roth? What are your goals to increase your contributions to hit your retirement goals?

- **Emergency Savings:** There's nothing like being able to go to sleep without fear. Especially knowing that if an emergency comes up, you have a financial plan to handle it. If you're an entrepreneur, you might consider having even more saved just in case. If you're risk-averse, you might also have a larger buffer. Set these goals, and make them happen and you'll sleep better at night.
- **Bucket List:** What experiences are on your bucket list that you want to achieve in your lifetime? Do you want to write and publish a book? Travel the world? Go back to school? Build out a savings plan with a timeline for your bucket list goals. Start saving for those goals and make them happen.

Still feeling lost? I recommend finding a financial planner you like and trust.

I check in with my financial planner at least once a year. And I have to say; I sleep better at night working with him. I know that I'm on track. I have a plan. I'm in a position to hit my goals. And that feels amazing.

STOP STRESSING ABOUT MONEY

Part of removing the stress around money is knowing what your financial goals are and building out a plan to make them happen. Once you have that in place, you'll feel a lot less stressed about money, even if you need to cut back on spending, even if you need to make more money. At least you know what you need to do.

But there's more to it than that. Even when I have a six- to twelve-month buffer. Even when I'm on track for retirement. Even when I have money to travel, sometimes I still feel anxious about money. And it used to be a lot worse.

I have spent years trying to remove that money stressor. Here's what has helped me.

When my money stress starts to come up in a big way, I pause to see what's really going on. It usually means something in my life is making me feel unsettled. I'm feeling unsafe, insecure, or there are some big changes coming my way.

It's not always about money. Money is closely tied to security and safety. Next time you feel stressed about money, stop and see if something else is being triggered.

It could be that you're afraid an intimate relationship is about to end. You could be worried about shifts in your business. It could be that you have a health trigger that's causing you stress. It could even be a minor life stressor that's bringing up old stuff.

Once you uncover what's going on, work with that. Address it. Make a plan. Then tell fear to stop driving. You've got this.

WORK ON YOUR MONEY MINDSET

A *huge* part of not stressing about money has to do with your mindset around money.

Each of us grows up with certain beliefs about money. They come from our childhood. Our parents, our family unit, and key people who were part of our lives influence how we see the world. And that includes how we see money.

If you grew up in a house where they were struggling to pay the bills or put food on the table, you're likely coming from a scarcity mindset. You probably put a great deal of weight on money. Perhaps you feel like you need it desperately.

If you grew up in a house where they had money but gave it away without much thought, you may find yourself struggling to manage a budget— struggling to manage your finances—wondering where the money went.

You get the idea. How you grew up and what those around you believed has likely influenced your money mindset.

So how do you shift that?

Recognize how you see money—what weight you put on it.

Consider these questions:

- Are you more prone to a scarcity or abundance mindset?
- Have you placed a glass ceiling on your success financially?
- Does the thought of money keep you up at night?

- Do you have trouble managing your finances?
- What beliefs do you have around money?
- What did your parents believe about money?
- What does your partner believe about money?

Those questions will help you assess where you are in your money mindset today. That's the first step to shifting it. Awareness.

Next, I want to challenge you with an exercise.

I want you to take out a piece of paper. I want you to imagine that money is not just an energetic thing or a paper bill. I want you to imagine that money is a person.

With that in mind, I want you to write a letter to money. I want you to tell money everything you think about it. I want you to write everything you want from money. I want you to tell money everything you believe about it. Don't hold back. Write everything and anything that comes to mind.

After you're done with the exercise, pause a moment. Then I want you to imagine you're the person, money. I want you to then read the letter you wrote to money as money.

As you read the letter as money, how does it make you feel?

While that sounds weird, trust me. Try that exercise. What comes up will be eye-opening. It will give you even more ideas for where you are with money—more insights on what you need to work on.

And if you get stuck, feel free to reach out. I'm here to help.

IMPROVE YOUR RELATIONSHIP WITH MONEY

If you did the exercise above, I guarantee you have some insights into your relationship with money.

You likely have some areas you can improve on.

For example, maybe you're putting all the pressure on money. Perhaps you aren't taking responsibility for your part. What can you do to shift that? How can you be in a better relationship with money?

Or perhaps you don't respect money. Perhaps you're angry with money. Perhaps you're afraid of what money will do to you. You believe money makes people monsters. What can you do to shift that perspective? How can you build respect for money? How can you release your anger?

Whatever it takes, money, like any relationship, has a significant impact on how you show up. If you're in sales or a business owner, it impacts your ability to sell. If you don't have a good relationship with money, your closing rate will likely be low or zero.

If you're afraid of money, you'll find that it's hard for you to hold onto money in your life. Or you'll find that you aren't making enough of it.

Can you see why that is so important to work on and shift?

Once you get right in your relationship and mindset with money, *big* shifts will start to happen. Let me know how it goes. I would love to hear from you!

BENEFIT 5—YOU'LL BE ABLE TO THINK CLEARLY AND REFOCUS

When you make self-care a priority, you'll feel centered, grounded, and have a better outlook on life.

When I'm *not* taking care of myself, I feel massive brain fog. Nothing is clear. I have to read and reread things several times.

When I'm talking with someone, I'm not able to listen fully. I get lost in the conversation because I'm not present. I'm in my head.

When I'm not making myself a priority, it shows up in my health in a massive way. I have more pain, migraines, less sleep, low energy, and I just don't feel like myself.

But when I do make my self-care a priority, I'm in "jetpack" mode. My friends call me Jetpack because I'm like an energizer bunny that gets sh*t done! When I'm centered, grounded, and taking care of myself, I'm ultra-productive.

I'm hitting my goals. I'm clear on what to say yes to. What to say no to. I'm focused on my priorities. I'm able to get everything important done and still have time to relax.

So, how can you build more clarity? How can you create the foundation for the focus and clarity I just described?

Here are some ways you can get started:

- *Build a daily routine.* I start every morning with meditation, visualization, affirmations, prayer, journaling, reading, and often, a workout. Your morning routine is very personal and specific to you. Experiment with what works for you.

  If you're having trouble getting started, check out my daily routine worksheet at https://coachhollyjackson.activehosted.com/f/34. It's a great starting point for you to experiment with what works for you.

  Don't get hung up on how much time you spend each morning. If you have a busy day, it could be two minutes. If you have more time, you could spend an hour in it. Just be sure to make it a habit. Do it every single morning, even if you're on vacation. The mornings I skip my routine are never as impactful. Never as productive. I'm off and not on my game when I skip it.

- *Plan your day and track your progress.* Years ago, I began to plan out my day the night before. I would block-schedule appointments, meetings, work I needed to complete, breaks, self-care items, and buffer time.

  Over time, I began to see the best time of day for me to do administrative work, creative work, client calls, etc. I was better able to set myself up for success in my schedule. I realized when days were overbooked and moved things before burning myself out.

  I also realized that having buffer time and flexibility are key. That way, if I'm not on my A-game, I can shift things around. If I don't feel well, I can focus more of my time on self-care, then tackle key things the following day.

  As I plan out my days, I like to grade them. At the end of the day, I like to acknowledge what I did well. Reflect on what I can improve. And grade the day on a five-star scale. Five being excellent. One being way off the mark. I consider days where I'm feeling off, and I move things to boost my self-care, a five-star day. It's not always about getting it all done. It's about how I did in terms of getting things done, scheduling in a reasonable way, being productive, and not feeling burnt out or overwhelmed. The more you do this, the more clarity and focus you'll have over time.

BENEFIT 6—YOU'LL FEEL HAPPIER AND MORE ACCOMPLISHED

Track your emotions. Start journaling and see how you feel on the days you take care of yourself. Compare that to how you feel on the days you let life run away with you. It happens to even the most practiced of us, but it's important to make self-care a priority even when life throws us curveballs.

Once you start tracking this, I guarantee you'll notice a positive trend tied to the days when you make yourself a priority. Self-care isn't just about physically taking care of your body.

There is a *huge* emotional component. Try doing one thing that boosts your self-care for seven days in a row and see how you feel. I bet you'll feel better and get surprisingly more done. When I prioritize myself, I feel great, have brilliant ideas, and get more done. And as you track your emotions, you'll also notice that they'll let you know when you need even more self-care. On the days when my emotions are strong or I'm feeling off, I know it means I need extra care.

Your emotions are like inner guides. They tell us when we are in flow and on track. And they tell us when we are out of alignment. When we are way off track, when something is wrong that we need to fix and deal with, we can't ignore those emotions. They're there to guide us. To help us. Even the ones that we don't want to feel have a purpose. Sadness is there to help us process and release. Fear is there to tell us we need to evaluate something. Anxiety is there to tell us something is awry.

Your emotions hold great value. Don't ignore them. Build a relationship with them. Get curious about them. You'll feel better for it.

Celebrate your success. We are not very good at celebrating success as humans. We are constantly busy setting that next goal. So busy, in fact, we don't even realize when we blast through the last one we set. It's important to pause and celebrate—to acknowledge our progress and success. Even if we're celebrating small milestones, pausing to acknowledge our progress is essential.

Life is about the journey. So why not make the journey fun? Why not celebrate every tiny milestone along the way? Doesn't acknowledging your progress make you feel more inspired, more joyful, happier? So, stop denying yourself the celebration. If you're trying to find a new job, celebrate landing that first interview. Celebrate writing your first resume. Celebrate applying to five jobs a day.

Enjoy the journey. You'll feel better for it. You'll wake up feeling inspired and motivated.

Not sure how to celebrate? It doesn't have to be big. It could be making a ritual every night of telling your partner three things you're proud of accomplishing. It could be journaling about the same. You could also create a celebrations list. A list of things you want to do to celebrate different milestones. Some of them could be small and some big. For example, I might treat myself to a pedicure for a small to medium-sized accomplishment. And for a bigger accomplishment, I might go on a trip with my partner. Make a list because then it will motivate you to hit your milestones and goals. And it will remind you to pause and celebrate the journey.

Pay it forward. Another way to enjoy the journey is to find ways to pay it forward. If you just hit a new milestone or learned something new that could help someone else, why not share it? I *love* doing webinars or talks for new business owners. Not all of them are paid or to find new clients. Some are simply to pay it forward because I believe that we all have the right to build the business of our dreams.

I believe each of us has a brilliant talent or idea to share with the world. What skills can you share with others? Paying it forward also makes you feel great. It will expand the circle of people in your world. You could find a mentee who needs your help. As a mentor, I find I learn more from my mentees than they learn from me. It's an interesting circle of life.

Find ways to pay it forward. Ways to give back to your community, your school, your company. You'll feel and be better for it.

BUILDING YOUR SELF-CARE MENU

Now that you're convinced that self-care is good for you and worth your time let's start building your self-care menu.

What is a self-care menu? It's a list of activities and things that help you feel supported, relaxed, and balanced. It's very personal. No one's self-care menu will be exactly the same as another's.

Some people love yoga and meditation for self-care. Others love exercise and hiking. And others find reading and quiet restorative. There is no wrong answer. The key is that only *you* can define what is on your menu.

EVALUATING SELF-CARE ACTIVITIES CHECKLIST:

- Does it make you feel better?
- Do you feel calmer and more grounded after?
- Are you able to process your emotions after doing this activity?
- Is it good for you physically and emotionally?

The activities you add to your self-care menu should all be yes to the questions above. Some of them may not help you process your emotions, but you should have some that do.

Make sure your menu is robust. It should help you deal with lots of challenging situations. There should be something on there that you can do anywhere, even when you're traveling. There should be something that will help you no matter what life throws your way.

Think of your self-care menu as your life raft. We want it to be really buoyant. That means you need activities that will help you get out of emergency situations. It shouldn't be too long either.

When life throws us a curveball, we can feel overwhelmed. If our menu is too long, we won't know where to start. Make sure your list is robust and focused.

HERE ARE SOME IDEAS FOR YOU:

- Yoga
- Meditation or Breathing Techniques
- Hiking or Camping
- Exercise (run, swim, cycle, etc.)
- Call a Close Friend
- Music (play or listen to it)
- Mani/Pedi

- Float
- Therapy or Life Coach Call
- A Walk in Nature
- Journaling

Still stuck?

Get your copy of my self-care menu worksheet for more ideas and a menu to start experimenting with: https://coachhollyjackson.activehosted.com/f/30

Consider the Health Secrets Master Class: https://hollyjeanjackson.com/healthsecrets as a companion to this book. It has worksheets, videos, and other tools to help you explore your self-care, your health foundation, and much more.

KEYS TO SUCCESS:

As you get started, it's important to **make this a daily task**. Otherwise, the habits won't stick. It takes 30-60 days to build a solid habit. Make self-care part of your daily routine.

Even if it's taking two minutes every morning to check in with yourself and see how you're feeling and doing something to shift that to feeling even better, that's something. The first step is awareness of how you're doing.

Schedule your self-care time. It helps you get started. You can start with five minutes each morning and then choose a couple of times throughout the week for twenty- to thirty-minute time blocks. Hold those appointments as sacred because they are. Do something for yourself from your self-care menu in those time blocks.

If you think you don't have time, you're wrong. Schedule what's important. Make space for it. If you're so busy you can't find time every day for self-care, your life is out of control. You need to refocus your priorities. Put yourself first.

Create a bedtime routine.

This will help you assess your progress and remind you to acknowledge it—to celebrate what has gone well. To hit pause and check in on how you're feeling and doing. Your bedtime routine is unique to you.

I like to start with two things I'm grateful for. Then I acknowledge two to three things I'm proud of accomplishing that day.

I like to check in with how I'm feeling from the day physically and emotionally. And I evaluate if I handled the day well. Did I take care of myself? Or just push through to get my to-do list done? What could I do better next time around? What do I need tomorrow?

Still stuck?

Here's my bedtime routine worksheet that I share with clients to help them get started: https://coachhollyjackson.activehosted.com/f/32

Use it to experiment with what works for you. Add to it. Play with it. Find what works best for you.

6

STRESS AND ANXIETY KILLS

*"Rule number one is, don't sweat the small stuff.
Rule number two is, it's all small stuff."*

~ ROBERT ELIOT

Stress *kills*.

Anxiety forces us into a vice of indecision over the fear of taking any action. Don't let stress or anxiety fool you. Don't let them take the steering wheel for your life. Take back the reins. Take charge of your life.

But first, let's explore what stress does.

Every single time I'm going through a stressful life circumstance, it shows up in my body. It shows up in my health. It wreaks havoc across my entire life . . . if I let it.

When I'm stressed out, I can't sleep. My eye starts twitching. My neck and shoulders get tense, creating havoc and pain—my body aches. I find myself getting new pains and injuries.

It has taken me years to figure out how to cope with my stress and anxiety.

I'm still not perfect. After experiencing multiple layoffs, moving several times, including across the country twice, and navigating a divorce, I have discovered a system that works.

I have faced some of the biggest stressors, many all at once, and made it through with less stress using this system.

I've had to navigate a divorce all alone while finding a new job and move to a new place. I've moved across the country alone during a pandemic.

I've been stung by a scorpion in the middle of the jungle in Guatemala. I thought I was going to die. We were four hours away from any major city and no one spoke much English. I will never forget explaining to the young man at our hotel in the middle of the night about what happened and him responding with, "Oh no!" Not reassuring. But I lived and it's a good story. It hurt like hell for at least 24 hours, but I lived.

While in Jamaica on a bus tour, our bus hit someone. We crashed and glass flew back into the seats we were sitting in. We were on the side of the road for hours wondering if we were safe. It was dark and raining in a foreign country. Very scary.

While traveling for work in India, I became very ill. I was alone and had to navigate a lot in a foreign place. I have a lot of allergies to medicines, so I refused to go to their hospitals. I emailed my doctor back in the states asking for his advice. He told me what to take over the counter and advised not to see a doctor there. The doctor that did visit my hotel room tried to prescribe me something that would have killed me due to allergies because medicines aren't the same in other countries. Luckily, I was smart enough to check on things. It was very stressful because I had to fly home with congestion and clogged ears. It felt like my head was going to explode the entire 21-hour journey home. I couldn't stop coughing. By the time I got home, I was so clogged up I had to crawl on the floor because I felt like I would pass out from the fluid in my ears.

I have faced stressors of varying degrees. Some small. Some big. The system I have put together works on any stressor you may be facing.

It's possible to navigate the stressors of modern society without it ruining your health or life.

My system will help you recognize when you're spiraling out of control due to stress and anxiety. My system will help you identify when you're in the spiral and how to stop the spiral. It will give you the tools to help you navigate through stress and anxiety.

With this system, you will have the tools you need to navigate any stressor with your head held high.

That's not to say you won't ever have a meltdown. Nor is it to say it won't be emotional. That's part of the experience.

When I was working for Visa, I was 100% loyal. I wanted to work there for the rest of my career. I loved their mission and vision. I loved working with my boss and team. So, when I was blindsided one day by a layoff, it was devastating.

That morning, I received an email from HR informing me that I would have a call with our team's senior director and HR online in an hour. I went to a private room as we were in open bench seating at the office. As I walked into the room, I could feel my heart racing. I felt anxious, stressed, and unsure. I got on the call. It felt like my throat was going to close. My hands trembled. My mind raced.

Nothing good comes from a call with HR. What did I do wrong? What was this about? Hold it together, Holly. They can't see you fall apart. Okay, let's just get through this call.

When I got on the call, my boss's boss and our senior director were both on the video conference line with me and HR. As I waited for someone to speak, I remember thinking, *this can't be good. Good God, are they firing me? Why? What for?*

Sean spoke calmly to me, "I really appreciate all your hard work but we have to make some cuts. Not just your position. Your entire team is being let go, including your boss, Casey. I'm so very sorry Miss Jackson."

As they began to outline what would happen next and what the severance package included, I could feel my whole world drop out from underneath me. I felt abandoned. I felt unsupported. I felt betrayed. I was so hurt and angry.

I was in shock. I held it together for the call, but as soon as I got off, I began to cry. And not just cry . . . I was sobbing. I was hyperventilating.

And it just continued to get worse.

I had to gather my things at once and be escorted from the building. Not only was I being let go, but I felt as though I was treated like a criminal.

It was one of the most embarrassing moments of my life. I wasn't able to hold it together, and people could see me at my weakest moment. They saw that I was upset. It was mortifying.

Because I was in the city and my home was on the other side of the bay, they paid for an Uber to pick me up and escorted me to the elevators.

The whole process happened within twenty to thirty minutes. Just like that, four years of hard work, and I was let go. I was no longer needed. I felt so used. I thought I had made myself a vital part of the team. Boy, was I wrong!

Layoffs, even when there is a nice severance package, are brutal. The problem is that we invest ourselves in companies. We give one hundred percent, yet you can never know if the company or your boss really has your back. Because companies are about numbers, they don't seem to understand that people are what make great companies.

Being treated like a number is demoralizing and inhumane. It triggers so many negative emotions. It makes you question your worth. It kills your confidence. It's not a fun experience. But it happens all the time. Over and over.

I sought out new tools to help me find a new way of living.

I found a yoga retreat and signed up. At that seven-day retreat, I learned tools for meditation, yoga nidra (breathing exercises to calm my nervous system), and yoga. It was exactly what I needed.

I felt so much better. I was finally grounded—present.

I made meditation part of my daily morning routine. I even continued to practice yoga every single day for at least thirty minutes. When I had trouble sleeping, I used practices like yoga nidra and breathwork to fall asleep naturally.

Because of the positive benefits of that yoga retreat, I decided I wanted to go even deeper. I wanted to learn everything I could about the tools.

I signed up for my 200-hour yoga teacher training mentorship with the same woman who led the yoga retreat I attended.

It was the best decision I ever made for my health. In my mentorship, I learned about the foundations for yoga. Yoga isn't just about movement. It's a way of living—a way of being.

I learned tolerance, integrity, self-discipline, nonviolence, non-stealing, spiritual growth, and much more. My teacher required that I spend a week on each yoga principle, journaling what it meant to me—how I would change my life to expand and grow.

That forced me to evaluate my life. To go inward. To reflect on the life I was living and how I wanted to live differently. I was able to grow. I felt more grounded, peaceful, and calm.

My family and friends could see the difference. I remember speaking with my mom one day and she told me, "Holly you have changed so much. I can hear how much calmer you are. You seem so much happier. I am so happy for you. So proud of you. I love you."

One of my closest friends shared with me over lunch, "Holly what have you done with yourself? You are absolutely glowing! It's like you've done a full-blown internal makeover. What's your secret?"

I didn't have trouble sleeping anymore. I didn't freak out as easily. I had tools to help me cope with stress and anxiety. I was able to manage my fear, anxiety, and stress in a whole new way. One that was never available to me before.

I felt empowered. Stronger. Like I could do anything.

If you're in a cycle or pattern that's not working, take pause. Ask yourself, "What can I do differently to get out of this? What tools do I need to break this vicious pattern?"

Getting tools that work for you to break the spiral is critical. Don't wait another day. Get the help you need. You're worth it.

In hindsight, I know that layoff from Visa was good for me. It was life's way of smacking me in the face and telling me, "What the hell are you doing?"

It forced me to break my pattern. To break old habits. Old ways of thinking.

It allowed me to pause and find solutions that worked. Through yoga, I was able to slowly shift my mindset. I was able to let go of limiting beliefs, old baggage, and a lot of anxiety.

And in stopping to work on myself, there were tons of other benefits.

I boosted my savings. My layoff gave me the tools and confidence that eventually led me to a new opportunity, starting my own business. It opened a lot of doors for me.

But in the moment, it felt like my world was closing in on me—like I would never get back on my feet.

So, how do we work with our stress and anxiety? How do we process experiences like that? How can we navigate situations like that without getting sick? How can we have a more peaceful experience with difficult life circumstances?

Let's dive into my system!

YOUR STRESS AND ANXIETY SYSTEM:

1. Break Free from Denial
2. Stop and Breathe
3. Go Inside
4. Identify Your Triggers
5. Build Your Toolkit
6. Use the System
7. Pass it On

Let's explore each of these.

STEP ONE: BREAK FREE FROM DENIAL

The reality is, we all have stress. It can be good stress or bad. Stress is stress. And what it does to our bodies is *bad* news. How we cope with it is the key.

If you're reading this chapter, it means you can do better. It means you're in the right place. You're ready to live a life free from stress ruling your life.

Stop pretending you don't have stress. Accept that it's part of life. And then commit to becoming aware of it and its impacts.

Still not convinced?

HERE ARE SOME DAUNTING STATISTICS ABOUT STRESS:

- About one-third of people around the world reported feeling stressed, worried, and/or angry in 2019 (Gallup)
- Approximately 284 million people worldwide have an anxiety disorder (Our World in Data, 2017)
- Nearly 1 in 5 American adults say that their mental health has declined since last year (American Psychological Association, 2020)
- US adults surveyed in 2020 reported that increased stress has:
  - Negatively affected their behavior (49%)
  - Increased tension in their bodies (21%)
  - Caused them to "snap" out of anger (20%)
  - Caused unexpected mood swings (20%)
- A 2017 study showed that the top causes of stress in America were:
  - Money (64%)
  - Work (60%)
  - The economy (49%)
  - Family responsibilities (47%)
  - Personal health problems (46%) (American Psychological Association, 2017)

THE PHYSICAL IMPACTS OF STRESS

The short-term physical symptoms of stress (reference: https://www.singlecare.com/blog/5-surprising-ways-stress-affects-your-body/) include headaches, muscle tension, fatigue, elevated heart rate, upset stomach, and trouble sleeping.

Mental health symptoms include irritability, restlessness, and lack of focus.

In the long run, consistently high stress levels can cause depression, anxiety disorders, gastrointestinal problems, sexual dysfunction (reference: https://www.singlecare.com/blog/stress-anxiety-and-erectile-dysfunction/), and weight gain. Prolonged stress has even been linked to heart disease. (reference: https://www.singlecare.com/blog/news/stress-statistics/)

If you still aren't convinced, simply search online for statistics around stress and its impacts on your physical and mental health. There is a plethora of information.

Whatever you do, get out of denial. Recognize that stress and anxiety are part of life, and the sooner you put together a system to cope, the better off you, your life, and your health will be.

Commit to the system. Keep reading. You've got this!

STEP TWO: STOP AND BREATHE

If we don't stop and check in with ourselves, we won't know how we are doing. How can you fix your stress if you don't even know it's there?

The key to overcoming stress is to have a heightened awareness of how you're feeling. That will allow you to become aware of when stress is wreaking havoc.

Here's a checklist you can use when you stop and breathe:

- **Stop wherever you are and close your eyes. Simply breathe.** Don't rush this. Go through each step. When you're first getting started, it may take longer.

- **Scan your body.** Are you tight anywhere? Are you feeling pain? Is your breathing deep or shallow? Are you tired?

- **Scan your emotions.** How are you feeling? Are you sad, happy, tired, energized? Don't judge any emotions. Simply identify how you're feeling.

- **Tune into your energy.** Imagine a ball of energy in your root chakra (near the base of your spine). Continue breathing into your personal energy. What does it feel like? As you continue breathing, try to expand your energy so that the ball of energy encompasses your entire body. Your personal energy should feel good.

- **Let go of anything negative.** If you're feeling anxious, stressed, fearful, or sad, try letting it go. As you expand your personal energy field, imagine anything negative melting away—melting out of your experience. If that doesn't work, we will dig into other tools that will help you let go in step five.

- **Consider building out your morning routine.** My morning routine consists of meditation, affirmation work, journaling, using spiritual cards to guide my intention for the day, visualization, and exercise. To build out a morning routine that works for you, check out my daily routine worksheet. Use it to experiment and explore a routine that works for you: https://coachhollyjackson.activehosted.com/f/34

STEP THREE: GO INSIDE

Now that you have paused to take stock of your physical and emotional state of being, it's time to go even further within.

Instead of resisting how we feel, it's crucial that we openly explore our emotions. If we ignore our emotions, they'll become pain, inflammation, or ailments within our bodies. By allowing them to be and exploring them, we are better able to find ways to process them.

Having heightened awareness around our emotions allows us to begin the process of healing—the process of releasing negative emotions.

If you're having trouble with your emotions, try journaling. Write down how you're feeling each morning. Write down where it's showing up in your body—how you're feeling physically from the emotion.

Whatever you do, learn how to uncover your emotions. Take the time to make it a daily priority.

Don't push them away. Don't ignore them. If you do, I guarantee, it will create something unhealthy and negative in your body.

BY DISCOVERING HOW TO BUILD A RELATIONSHIP WITH
OUR EMOTIONS AND FEELINGS, WE ARE BETTER ABLE TO
DETERMINE WHEN WE ARE IN A SPIRAL.

You can then become aware when you are spinning out of control. Becoming aware of when our emotions are dictating actions, allows you to choose differently.

The reality is that emotions pass. "Motion" is part of the word emotion for a reason. Emotions, even strong ones, pass. They last minutes, not forever.

Learning to sit with emotion is critical. It allows us to show up in a calmer state of mind. It helps us have better communication, not dedicated to a passing emotion.

Emotions are also a signal. They can tell us that something is wrong—that we are out of alignment. If you're repeating a cycle of a strong negative emotion with a partner, it's a sign that you need to get help for your relationship. Or it's a sign that it's not a good fit.

Either way, it's helpful information and a sign for you to take action when you're in a calm state of mind. Not in a heightened emotional state. Most regret comes from people making decisions based on emotion . . . in the moment when it's strongest.

Fixing our spiral and how we deal with stress and anxiety is an inside job. Any kind of healing is a very personal journey. It requires that we each go inside of ourselves. We each experiment with and find the tools that work for us.

That is why step five is so important. You will build out your personal toolkit in that step. No one else's toolkit will be the same.

No one experiences stress the same way you do. You're unique and valuable. Take the time to explore and reflect on it. It's worth it because you're worth it.

STEP FOUR: IDENTIFY YOUR TRIGGERS

Now that you have learned how to pause and go deep within, it's time to begin identifying your triggers.

And if you're thinking, *I don't have any,* go back to step one, breaking denial.

We all have triggers. You know you're being triggered when you have a strong emotional response to something small. You know you're triggered when it's bringing up junk from the past. You know it's a trigger when it takes you back to your childhood or a traumatic situation. You're being triggered when you can't remain calm or let the emotion pass—when you're unable to center yourself.

It's important to identify your triggers because awareness is the first step to transformation of any sort. If you know and understand your triggers, it's easier to step back and look at the situation.

When you understand what's happening, it allows you to get more distance. More space. More ability to control what you do with the information and how you will react.

Here are some questions for you to reflect on and journal about to identify your triggers:

- What are your stress and anxiety triggers?
- What pushes your buttons?
- What happens when you're triggered?
- How does it show up in your body?
- What are you thinking?

My biggest triggers are as follows:

- My health. New injuries. Sickness. Pain.
- Not feeling heard. Someone interrupting me or not really listening to me.
- Fear of being abandoned. A friend or significant other leaving me or my life. Someone close pulling away physically or emotionally.
- Feeling trapped. Not having an exit route from uncomfortable situations. Feeling emotional in a situation I can't get out of.
- Inappropriate sexual advancements. Catcalling from men. Imposing moves.

Knowing your triggers will help you navigate your stress and anxiety. It will allow you to take back some control. You will be better equipped to handle your emotions. And they'll feel more intense when you're triggered.

Take the time to explore your triggers. The list will grow and change with time, so be sure to revisit it occasionally.

Share your triggers with loved ones and your partner. Share with them what you need when you're triggered. That will help you have better communication and more intimacy.

STEP FIVE: BUILD YOUR STRESS AND ANXIETY TOOLKIT

What do we do when we are triggered or feeling stress or anxiety?

That's unique to each person. So, let's explore how to build out your stress and anxiety toolkit.

Here are some questions to consider:

- What activities help you relax?
- When you're angry, what helps you feel calm and safe?
- When you're upset, what do you need?
- When you're experiencing loss or grief, what activities or things do you need to process?
- What things and activities bring you the most joy and peace?
- What hobbies or exercises put you into a state of flow (where time passes by rapidly)?

Some Ideas to Consider:

- Yoga or meditation
- Exercise (swim, run, dance, hike, bike, weight lift, kickboxing, etc.)
- A walk with a good friend
- Coffee with a loved one
- Cuddling up with a good book
- Watching a funny movie with a cup of tea
- Being in nature (sitting in the grass, going to a park, hiking)
- Breathing (any kind of breathwork that grounds you)
- Journaling

- Screaming into a pillow
- Speaking or venting to a friend

There are no right or wrong answers. It simply needs to work for you.

My stress and anxiety list varies depending on the situation. That is why it's important to have a *big* list. That way, you have something that works for any situation.

When I'm angry, I need to run, kickbox, scream into a pillow, or be outside. When I'm sad, I need hugs, cuddles, and time with loved ones. When I'm grieving, I need to play the piano, spend time with friends, exercise, breathe, journal, and do a lot of yoga. When I'm triggered by my health, I need yoga, breathwork, to speak with my life coach, and to work on affirmations and mindset.

Knowing what will help you process and become calm again is helpful. And knowing your triggers and which tools will help you most, given a situation, empowers you.

You know how to handle anything life throws you.

Still stuck?

Check out my Stress and Anxiety Toolkit worksheet: https://coachhollyjackson.activehosted.com/f/17

STEP SIX: USE THE SYSTEM

Any time a stressor shows up, use the system. You have the awareness and tools to cope. Don't forget to use them.

Don't make this mistake. You get to a place where you aren't freaking out or spiraling as often. You might slack on one of the steps. Perhaps you let the daily routine drop. Or you think, *I don't need that toolkit. I've got this. I've mastered my stress.*

If you do that, it will blow up in your face.

How do I know? I've done it. Whenever I think I've got this under control and I drop a step, it never works. My stress gets out of control. I start to spiral. And I wonder, what happened?

I dropped the system.

Don't make this mistake. Stick to the program. It's worth it.

Since we aren't in denial now, we know stress is part of life. Don't fall back into denial. Don't get lazy. Don't get cocky, thinking you have your stress under control (not using the system).

Stick to the system; it works. But you have to take action tied to the system for it to help—every single day.

STEP SEVEN: PAY IT FORWARD

Share it with others who also suffer from stress and anxiety. Help them break free.

When I'm helping others, it makes me feel even better.

When I'm coaching a client, it puts me into a state of flow. In fact, I love to start my days with writing, followed by coaching. That puts me into the right state of mind and the right energy to have an amazing day!

Paying it forward could even be in your toolkit. It might help you feel calmer. It won't hurt. It could even improve your mood and your outlook. Give it a try.

Don't forget, go back to step one and continue to repeat the process.

It's a daily process. It's something you will continue to work on for life.

If we aren't growing and learning, we are slowly dying. Don't be a zombie. Don't give up on life. Don't let your emotions and circumstances rule you.

Take back your power. Use your gifts. Make the world a better place, starting with *you*!

You've got this!

7

SHIFTING OUR SELF-TALK AND MENTAL HEALTH

"If we can change our thoughts, we can change the world."

~ H.M. TOMLINSON

Do you ever find yourself sitting with a loved one, and they ask you, "Hey, are you there?" It happens to us all. We do our best to remain present, but our thoughts take over.

Our thoughts are like tidal waves—tugging at us, pulling us away from the present moment.

Our mental chatter can keep us from intimacy, good communication, and enjoying life. When we let our self-talk take the steering wheel for our lives, we are living like zombies.

So how can you take back control? Live in the present moment? And fix the negative thought patterns and cycles you're stuck in?

Let's start by defining self-talk.

WHAT IS SELF-TALK?

The things we think about ourselves, who we are, how we feel, and how others see us are a big part of self-talk.

For example, when you respond to a trigger from a loved one, are you saying to yourself, "I am terrible at communicating. I suck. That was terrible. What's wrong with you?! He is going to leave you. You don't deserve to be in a relationship."

You get the picture. Are you spiraling into a downward path of negative thoughts? If so, that is negative self-talk. And it happens all the time, even in the best of circumstances.

I remember last week; my partner and I were at a secluded beach in Costa Rica. It was a perfect day. Gorgeous weather. We were getting along wonderfully. We found the perfect spot on the beach. And he went to swim. We saw signs about how dangerous the rip currents can be.

While he was swimming, my mind wandered.

What if a current gets him? Can I save him? What would I do? We aren't near anyone with access to emergency services. What would I do? What if I die going after him?

That went on for a couple of minutes before I caught myself in the old habit. Then, I was able to reset my thoughts and mindset.

Most of us aren't even aware that we are spiraling half the time. So, our thoughts pull us like those dangerous riptides I read about. They pull us away from the joy of the moment. They keep us from being present. They steal those moments from us. We miss out on opportunities for connection, growth, and contentment.

Self-talk can also show up in regular day-to-day moments. They don't have to pull us into a spiral for them to have a negative impact.

I can be sitting at dinner with my partner having a perfectly wonderful evening, and then a thought pops into my head. He has a look of dissatisfaction on his face. Instead of checking in with him to see what's going on, my mind wanders.

What did I do or say that upset him? Is there something in my teeth? What if he is tired of me? Am I losing him? Does he not want to be here with me?

These small moments happen to us all the time. The problem is when the thoughts are far from reality. And when they're negative.

A lot of our self-talk is based on beliefs from our childhood, most of which are no longer true. Those old limiting beliefs are not serving us as adults. But most of us are not even aware we have them.

LIMITING BELIEFS AND SELF-TALK

How do you identify your limiting beliefs?

Begin by listening to and tuning into your thoughts. Write down on paper when thoughts pop into your mind. Especially the ones that are tied to intense responses or emotions.

Do you see any patterns or loops in these thoughts that are surfacing? Do any of them have to do with the same thing?

For example, I've had work to shift my beliefs when it comes to my body. Since I was little, I have had a lot of fear around health and safety. My mom was sick when I was young. She had multiple surgeries and then was diagnosed with multiple sclerosis, a disease where the immune system eats away at the protective covering of the nerves. Growing up with that made me fearful and paranoid about my health.

I also grew up in a household where sharing your emotions wasn't welcome. It was frowned upon to cry or show sadness. My mom would say, "Holly Jean, there's no reason for tears. You have so much to be grateful for. Turn that frown upside down. Look at the bright side. There's always a bright side. Besides you must be strong. You are so much stronger than you realize."

We were supposed to be happy all the time—to put on a happy face in public even if we were dying inside. As a very sensitive and emotional being, I had to learn how to hide myself—to hide my feelings and my very strong emotions—to put on many masks and hide my vulnerability. It was exhausting.

When I failed and did show emotion, I was shamed. I was told there was something wrong with me, that I was too sensitive. Too emotional. Too much. Hearing that as a child severely impacted my confidence. It made me question myself. I, too, began to believe there was something seriously wrong with me as a human.

At five, I ended up having a kidney infection that was so bad I could not walk. I said, "Mommy, I really don't feel good. Everything hurts. I feel sick." I kept telling her this but she wasn't listening. She said, "Honey you're fine. You'll feel better." But when I couldn't walk, she said, "Okay Honey, we need to go see the doctor now." We went to the doctor's office and I remember the doctor pulling her aside and them whispering. I felt so scared. *What were they talking about? Was I a bad girl? Was I really sick? What was wrong with me?*

Then my mom came over and said, "We need to go to the hospital. Daddy will meet us there with your things. The doctors need to run some more tests to help make you feel better." I was hospitalized for a week. I was really sick. It was a scary situation that I remember to this day.

That, along with my other circumstances growing up, led me to believe the following:

- That we live in a dangerous, unsafe world
- That health is fragile
- That there was something wrong with me
- That I couldn't share my feelings because it wasn't safe to do so
- That being emotional is bad
- That expressing myself is dangerous
- That it was safer to put on a mask and pretend everything was great
- That asking for help showed great weakness

It took me years to uncover those limiting beliefs. I worked with therapists, life coaches, and an energy healer. I am still working on healing those old wounds—to up-level my belief system.

Even with all that hard work, sometimes those old thoughts and beliefs come back up when I am triggered by a deep wound from the past. But now, I know how to break free from those patterns when they resurface.

Not all limiting beliefs are apparent in adulthood until something big happens.

THE DIVORCE RABBIT HOLE

When I went through my divorce, a lot of my childhood stuff came up.

I remember thinking . . .

I am a failure. How can everyone else have a successful marriage, and yet I can't? I have failed at life. My husband is right; I am a terrible communicator.

There is something wrong with me. I am too much. I will never have a successful relationship. I am fat, ugly, unworthy. What will people think about me?

Will my church reject me? Will my friends and family judge me? How will I ever look at myself in the mirror again?

Can I survive this? Am I strong enough?

Sadly, my marriage was extremely verbally abusive. I experienced damaging comments for years from someone who I thought loved me dearly. Because of that, I slowly lost my identity.

What he told me about myself became my thoughts . . . then my beliefs . . . and then part of my identity. It took me years to undo the damage from that toxic relationship.

But I also learned the dangers of codependency and how to avoid it. I uncovered my part in it. I promised myself I would never let another human treat me that way ever again. I did the work to get better. To heal myself. To shift my negative thinking and find myself again.

If you're going through a divorce or breakup, I am here to tell you you're not a failure. You're not alone. You can survive this. You'll grow from this. This is not the end of your story. You can and will heal. You may feel lonely now, but this too will pass.

I urge you to take the time you need to heal—the time you need to uncover what you want to improve about yourself before your next relationship. Take time to reflect on what was your part of what went wrong in the marriage? And make a plan to grow and learn from it before you start dating again.

Before you start dating, make sure you're one hundred percent in love with yourself. Be sure you love every aspect of you. Your body. Your feelings. Your flaws. Your ticks. If you don't love yourself, wait to get back out there.

If you don't take the time to heal and love you first, you'll likely fall into a similarly flawed relationship, whether it's abusive, following a similar pattern or cycle, or doomed to end.

As you go through the healing process, reflect on your thoughts—your limiting beliefs. Do you believe you're worthy of love? Do you believe you're loveable? Do you believe you deserve a relationship that lasts? One that's better than the last one?

Uncover your limiting beliefs, then take the time to rewrite them. Break the barriers, limits, or walls you have placed around yourself. There is no box that fits anyone. There is only love and endless possibility.

Take the time. Heal. Grow. Love yourself.

THE BODY RABBIT HOLE

This limiting belief and thought cycle deserves its own section because I know too many people who struggle with this. Women and men are equally impacted by it.

I want to challenge you to a quick exercise. Take a piece of paper and write down everything you think about your body.

- What do you think about your size and shape?
- Are you happy with your hair?
- Do you love your legs?
- What are your least favorite things about your body?
- What do you love most about your body?
- When you look at yourself in the mirror before you leave to go on a date, what thoughts are running through your mind?

Unless everything you wrote down is 100% positive, you have room to improve your self-talk about your body. We all do.

We live in a society where there is a lot of pressure to look good. And what's defined as "good" is not accessible to everyone. Nor is it necessarily how others define beauty.

Identify what you dislike about your body. Identify the most common negative thoughts you have about your body. Write them down.

That will allow you to identify the areas you need to shift around your body.

How we see ourselves impacts the rest of our mindset. It affects how we show up at work. With our families. When we are dating. How we are with our partner.

Imagine how much better your life would be if you loved your body. Every single part of it. Even what you consider to be "flaws."

Wouldn't you show up at work more confident? Wouldn't your sex life be incredible? Wouldn't it be easier to negotiate for that raise or promotion at work? Imagine how much easier life would be if you loved every part of you.

And it goes beyond that. I want you to love every aspect of your personality, whether you're emotional and sensitive or you're strong and stoic.

The goal of self-talk is to get you to a place where you love 100% of yourself. It will increase your happiness and joy in life. It will reduce your stress, anxiety and pain. You'll be happier, more confident, and more successful.

So how do we shift our self-talk?

SHIFT YOUR SELF-TALK

Here are the steps to shift your self-talk. Please keep in mind that this work is ongoing. It's a lifetime journey.

There are always new layers to break through and improve. There are always new thought patterns that need shifting. There are new triggers that can bring up old stuff you thought you were healed from.

Be sure to stick to the program. Keep doing the work. I guarantee it's worth it.

SELF-TALK TRANSFORMATION STEPS

This process is easy to remember as it spells out, I see ups. As you take on this self-talk transformation journey, things can only improve from here!

- **Identify** your thought patterns
- **Categorize** your thought patterns into buckets (i.e., body image, relationships, health, work, etc.)
- **Uncover** your limiting beliefs
- **Prioritize** the thought patterns and limiting beliefs you need to fix first
- **Shift** your self-talk (i.e., thoughts and limiting beliefs) using the tools in this book

Now that you know the transformation steps let's dig into each one in more detail.

IDENTIFY YOUR THOUGHT PATTERNS

The first step into healing our self-talk is to become aware of the dialogue. To do this, you need to make time to pause and check in.

BELOW ARE SOME QUESTIONS FOR REFLECTION:

- What are you thinking about events or the situation you're in?
- What are you thinking about yourself and those around you?
- What judgments are you making in your mind?
- What emotions are tied to the thoughts you're thinking (i.e., how are you feeling when you think each thought)?
- When you're stressed, anxious, or feeling panicked, what thoughts are racing through your mind?
- What thoughts do you have repeatedly (good and bad)?
- Are there any thoughts that you find surprising or scary?
- Do you like how you talk to yourself (i.e., would you speak to a good friend the way you speak to yourself)?

Journal on these from time to time throughout the day. See what patterns begin to show up. Are there any specific thought loops you found to be surprising? Approach this exercise with openness and curiosity.

DON'T JUDGE YOURSELF FOR THINKING NEGATIVE THOUGHTS. JUDGMENT LIMITS YOUR GROWTH AND IS TOXIC IN YOUR TRANSFORMATION JOURNEY.

If you find a thought disgusting, simply think, *that's an interesting thought*, and let it float by like a cloud. Release it.

Thoughts only have power when we grasp onto them. They lose their power when we acknowledge them and let them float by. They're fleeting.

They gain power when we think certain thoughts repeatedly—when they turn into habits or actions.

That is why doing this work is so important. So, we can shift our thoughts . . . then our habits . . . then our beliefs . . . and finally, our identity.

BUCKET YOUR THOUGHT PATTERNS INTO CATEGORIES

As you continue to uncover your thoughts, begin placing them into buckets or categories. Any thoughts you have about your body or body image put into one bucket. Thoughts related to your worldview go in a separate bucket.

POSSIBLE THOUGHT PATTERN BUCKETS:
- Body image
- Relationships
- Communication
- Health
- Wealth and money
- Worldview
- Safety
- Work and Career
- Spirituality

Bucketing our thoughts can help us begin to uncover patterns and relationships. It might even help you discover the root cause of a limiting belief.

You can use Post-it Notes and group thoughts together. You could use tools like digital sticky notes or mind mapping tools to help you connect everything, whatever works best for you.

The important thing is to continue to uncover your thoughts. Build your awareness. Begin to discover what patterns or connections exist. That will help you with healing and transformation.

IDENTIFY YOUR LIMITING BELIEFS

Once you have your thought patterns in buckets, it will make this section much easier. The difference between a thought and a belief is important to understand.

A *thought* is something that can come and go. It could just be a really outlandish thought or a creative, imaginative idea. Not every thought rings true. Not every thought will be something you believe. Thoughts, once again, are often like clouds passing us by.

A *belief* is something you believe to be true about yourself, others, your experience, or the world.

For example, you may believe the world is an unsafe place, so you approach life from a stance of fear and trepidation. Or you may look at life as flowing, supportive, and loving. What you believe about the world impacts how you approach experiences, relationships, and life.

> WHAT YOU BELIEVE ABOUT YOURSELF WILL IMPACT THE VERY CORE OF WHO YOU ARE. YOUR BELIEFS CREATE YOUR IDENTITY.

That is why uncovering our limiting beliefs is so important. When we uncover them, we can begin to shift them to better beliefs—ones that support us in our adult life.

Most of our limiting beliefs are formed before the age of five. Our childhood experiences impact our thoughts, beliefs, and identity in ways that can last into adulthood.

QUESTIONS TO HELP UNCOVER LIMITING BELIEFS:

- As you look over your thought buckets, which ones are tied back to stories or experiences from your childhood?
- Can you see how some of your thoughts about life, relationships, and the world are influenced by childhood experiences?
- Do some of those beliefs seem to be untrue now that you're an adult?
- Do you dislike any of them?
- Are they placing a glass ceiling on your life?

If you said yes to any of the above or identified anything tied back to childhood, those are your core beliefs.

Another way to check in and uncover the strongest limiting beliefs is to look back over your list of beliefs and say each one out loud.

One at a time, notice how you feel when you say it. If you feel good, it's a good core belief. If you feel awful or sick to your stomach, then it's a limiting belief. The stronger the negative feeling, the more limiting it is, and the more you need to do the work to transform it.

The ones that feel the strongest in the negative sense are the ones you want to shift first. Some may be good. Some will be holding you back. The ones that are holding you back are the ones we want to focus on.

EXAMPLES OF LIMITING BELIEFS:

- The world is an unsafe place. I am not safe.
- I can't show my emotions. I can't be myself. If I do, people will think I am weak and will take advantage of me.
- I am too much. People can't handle me. I will never find a partner in life.
- I am unworthy of love and affection. I am not good enough.
- There is something wrong with me. I am unhealthy. I have health problems and injuries all the time.
- Bad things happen to me. I am like a magnet for bad accidents.
- I am ugly. I hate my body.

- I will never have enough money. I can't make it on my own. Money seems to escape me. People steal money from me easily.

- I will always be alone.

- People always leave me. I can't rely on others. The only person I can trust is myself.

Those were my *big* limiting beliefs. It's an ongoing battle. Most of them don't haunt me nearly as much as they did in the past. I have freedom.

I now have new beliefs that serve me. Beliefs that help me expand and grow. Thoughts and beliefs that allow me to be present. To be the best version of myself.

I promise you can get there too. Keep reading on. This section is one of the hardest to work through. Don't give up. The tools are coming up next.

You've got this. And you're worth it! I believe in you.

PRIORITIZE THE THOUGHT PATTERNS AND LIMITING BELIEFS TO FIX FIRST

Now that you know your limiting beliefs, you need to prioritize which ones have the biggest impact on your life.

Here are some ways you can begin to prioritize your list:

- Sit with each limiting belief, one at a time. See how you feel. On a scale of 1 to 10 (10 being the worst), how bad does it make you feel?

- When you reflect on each limiting belief, can you see how it's impacting the decisions you make, the thoughts you have, and the actions you take (i.e., in your finances, relationships, health, and life)?

- Is there one limiting belief in particular that consumes most of your thoughts (i.e., you obsess about it, stress over it, or go into an anxious rabbit hole frequently because of it)?

- Which limiting belief feels the most overwhelming to work on or think about?

Those questions should help you uncover your top one to three limiting beliefs. The one that makes you feel the worst and consumes the most of your thoughts is the one you'll want to target first. It's important to choose one or two to start working on.

If you try to fix them all at once, you'll likely be unsuccessful. It will be too overwhelming. Shifting too much of our identity at once will make the ego push back.

Transformation is impossible when our egos are heightened. Because the ego is there to keep us safe. Take this process step by step—one limiting belief at a time.

The next section will give you the tools you need to begin shifting your thoughts and beliefs.

Just like in the movie *What About Bob*, it's all about "baby steps . . . baby steps to the elevator." This process takes time. Be kind and gentle with yourself. You'll have setbacks. As long as you keep working the process, healing will come. I promise.

TOOLS TO SHIFT SELF-TALK

TOOL 1—WORK WITH A LIFE COACH OR THERAPIST

Explore and research what kind of therapist or coach is best for you. For example, there are cognitive-behavioral therapists who help you rewire your thinking. They help you dig into your thought patterns, your behaviors, and they help you shift them.

There are multitudes of life coaches with various areas of expertise. There are coaches certified in transformational coaching methodology. That means they can help you explore your childhood experiences that created your belief system. They can help you shift and transform your thoughts, beliefs, and identity with various tools.

I have worked with a cognitive-behavioral therapist to heal from past traumas and work on my chronic pain. I have also worked with a few transformational coaches, an energy healer, and a shaman to explore childhood beliefs and past lives. All have been incredibly helpful.

I find that working with a life coach, an energy healer, and my business coach is the right mix for me to stay on track.

Even after years of work, healing is an ongoing journey. There are always new layers for growth. New things to release and let go of. New levels of forgiveness.

Whatever mix you choose, be sure to find someone to work with. That kind of work can be unnerving and emotional. It's important to have a support system to walk this journey with you. Doing this work alone can be dangerous. Find someone you trust and with who you have good chemistry to guide you through the process.

TOOL 2—GET DISTANCE FROM YOUR THOUGHTS

Here are some tools you can use to get distance from your thoughts.

- **Stop and breathe.** Take at least one minute to breathe. Thoughts are fleeting. Sometimes taking a minute to breathe is all it takes to break the cycle.

- **Journal.** Write down what you're feeling, thinking, and emoting. Get it out of your body and onto paper. Getting it out of your mind will free you. It can help bring you peace. It absolutely gives you some distance because you can see it on paper versus just playing on repeat in your mind.

  Sometimes, I like to write a letter to a person, to God, even to money, and tell them everything I think. Maybe I'm angry. Maybe I want closure. Whatever it is, I write it out, and then I burn it. I don't need them to read it. I just need to get it out of my body. Out of my head.

- **Take a Break.** Do something that gets you out of your head and into your body. Go on a run, a hike, or dance in your living room. Do something to break the cycle. Watch a funny movie or call a close friend. Take care of you.

TOOL 3—THE STORY I AM TELLING MYSELF

Have you ever caught yourself telling an elaborate story in your head about the future or the past or what the person you're with is thinking about you? Then, you check in with that person, and it's *way* off track? It's not even close to what they're thinking or experiencing. And yet you're stressing yourself out, making up this elaborate story that you're experiencing in your head.

If this happens to you, stop, and use this tool.

Next time you're thinking of an elaborate story about what might happen to you or what your loved one is thinking, check in.

Say, "Hey, here's the story I am telling myself right now. I am telling myself that you're angry with me because you seem a little off this morning. And I am thinking to myself that I have done something wrong, that you're angry with me. Is that true, or is something else going on?"

I guarantee, 99% of the time, the story you're telling yourself is *wrong*—dead wrong.

Instead of stressing and going down the rabbit hole, creating multiple ludicrous stories about the future, just check in. Save yourself the grief. When you check in, you're saving yourself a lot of grief.

So many arguments and miscommunications occur from stories we tell ourselves. They're almost always figments of our imagination.

Use this tool to check in with yourself too. You could be thinking that something bad is going to happen.

Talk out loud to yourself or journal. Is this something that's likely to happen? If it did, I would be fine. And let it go. Get back to the present moment.

Don't let these stories pull you away from the present. Don't let them steal life from you.

TOOL 4—AFFIRMATIONS

One way you can begin shifting your thoughts and beliefs is by using affirmations. Affirmations are statements that start with "I am." They're stated in the present tense.

For example, if you have a limiting belief that says, "I am ugly. I hate my body," you could use an affirmation like, "I am grateful for the activities my body allows me to do. I am working on seeing my own beauty."

You don't want the affirmation to be so far from the truth that you can't believe anything about it.

Write out your biggest limiting belief and begin experimenting with affirmations that feel good to you. That helps you begin shifting your belief in the right direction.

There are many affirmation tools and apps out there. Find what works best for you.

Look at your affirmations every day—multiple times a day. Say them out loud to yourself in the mirror until you believe them.

Once you believe them, up-level your affirmation to something even more empowering. Once you love your new belief in that one area, move to the next limiting belief, and work on it.

Need help?

Download my affirmations worksheet: https://coachhollyjackson.activehosted.com/f/42

TOOL 5—NIGHTTIME RITUALS

Consider taking time every night to list three things you're grateful for that day. Make sure one thing you're grateful for has to do with yourself.

Write down or share out loud with your partner two things you're proud of accomplishing that day. We as a society are not good at acknowledging progress. Doing this every night will make it easier for you to build your confidence, be more present, and celebrate your wins.

Make this a ritual.

Unplug an hour before bedtime. That will help you connect with family and yourself. It will help you feel more grounded. It will allow you to be more present. And you'll fall asleep faster and get better quality sleep.

Give it a try. It will help your mental health in *big* ways.

Need a reminder?

Download my Bedtime Worksheet today: https://coachhollyjackson.activehosted.com/f/32

TOOL 6—STRATEGIES TO SHIFT SELF-TALK CHEAT SHEET

Download my cheat sheet as a reminder of all the strategies you can use to shift your self-talk. Anywhere, anytime: https://coachhollyjackson.activehosted.com/f/44

No matter what you do, never stop growing. Never stop exploring your thought patterns, feelings, beliefs, and experiences with curiosity.

The day we stop growing is the day we start digging our grave.

I want you to thrive and soar!

Put in the work, baby step after baby step, and you'll reach even higher highs, higher peaks, and bigger joy.

You've got this!

Now that we have talked about internal work and our mental health let's dive into our physical health.

8

MOVE YOUR BODY!

*"We don't stop playing because we grow old;
we grow old because we stop playing."*

~ GEORGE BERNARD SHAW

Since I was a little girl, I was blessed with a willingness and passion for movement and exercise. I have always enjoyed being on the go—from swim team to running, from hiking to spinning, whatever it was, I had to be moving.

That is how I eventually got the nickname "Jetpack."

When I have a new injury from overdoing something or aging, my doctors have to tell me to take it easy. And I have to ask them to define what that means. Otherwise, I will go out and bike fifty miles, swim two miles and run six miles and lift weights which is my usual routine.

I can't say that I am the norm because I thrive on and *love* my endorphin hits. I am almost; one could say, addicted to being active, especially getting those endorphin highs, which only come from really pushing myself in the pool, on the bike, or running. There is nothing quite like it.

For all my runners here reading this, you get what I mean. It's that buzz that starts to kick in and vibrates throughout your entire body. It brings you joy. You smile. You get that rush and burst of energy, and it allows you to run further and faster. And it's *fun*! There is nothing in this world like it.

So, we find ourselves chasing that next high.

Even when I had my ten-level spinal fusion, I will never forget that they had me up and about, walking the same day they operated.

MOVEMENT IS PART OF THE HEALING PROCESS. IT IS PART OF THE HUMAN EXPERIENCE.

When I was participating in pain clinics for my back before my surgery, one thing they all promoted was movement. Walking, they said, was helpful for spine pain. "Avoid sitting and being still for long periods of time," they said.

And they were right. Walking and even gentle movement throughout the day is a *huge* needle mover for managing pain.

To this day, when I get a cold, and I lose my workout routine, other pain crops up. Movement for me is one of the most healing pieces of my puzzle. It is a necessary part of my daily routine. Without it, I am in significantly more pain.

THE PROBLEM WITH EXERCISE

Not all of us are blessed with a natural need for movement. Some of us struggle with it.

There's also a negative connotation that comes with exercise for many. That is why I like to talk about movement instead.

Exercise gets a bad rap. It's right up there with dieting. No one wants to be told what to do when it comes to their body. We want options. We want it to be fun. We want flexibility.

When I work with clients on their health, and we talk about exercise, a wall goes up. They get defensive—their energy changes.

But when I talk with clients about movement, something different happens. They get curious. They say, "What do you mean by movement?" And that's exactly what we want when we design our movement menu. Fun!

We want to make moving our bodies a pleasurable experience. Not painful. Not creating resistance or struggle. So, why not start your morning by dancing for five minutes to your favorite song? It's a great way to wake up, start the day, and have fun while moving.

Or perhaps try starting a neighborhood walking group at lunchtime. Walk together to build community while moving your body.

You could even create a "mommy and me" yoga group with other local moms who want to move with their children. Make it fun, gentle, and inviting.

To begin your experimentation with movement, you could even find meetup groups around hobbies you enjoy, like swimming, cycling, hiking, and traveling.

If that's not your thing, play catch at the dog park with your dog. Have a movement party with your family while you clean the dishes. Walk the stairs instead of taking the elevator. Have a ten-minute movement session with your coworkers and have someone new lead it every day.

Whatever you do, find some form of movement that works for you. If you are having trouble building your movement menu, check out my movement worksheet here: https://coachhollyjackson.activehosted.com/f/54

GET OUT OF THE DOLDRUMS

I remember watching a movie called *The Phantom Tollbooth* as a child. And in the book and movie, there's a place called the Doldrums. When I look at unhealthy people, they are usually stuck in the Doldrums.

They have a mental block that's limiting them. They refuse to move. They are stuck in their misery. The longer they hang out in the Doldrums, the more broken down they become. The more lost, lonely, desperate, and in pain they become.

It's difficult to get into action when you're in the Doldrums because the creatures that live there, much like our negative thinking, talk you down. They say, "You don't need to move" or, "You'll never get better, so what's the point" or, "What's the point in trying anything; it never works." Don't let the Doldrums fool you.

The only way out is to get up and get moving. To refuse to listen to them. To know there is another way forward.

Our bodies are built for movement. Back in caveman days, women would gather and watch the children while the men hunted. We stayed fit and active out of necessity to survive. Many of those natural ways of living have been lost to us in modern society.

It's important to remember that we are built for movement. Even if we don't require it to survive, the body and mind feel better when we use them properly.

We are not designed to sit on a couch and binge-watch movies or TV shows. We are designed to be active and engaged in communities, sitting in circles by the campfire, sharing stories about survival and thriving—learning from one another.

Movement is essential.

WHEN WE DON'T MOVE OUR BODIES, THINGS START TO BREAK. WE GET NEW INJURIES OR PAIN IN OUR BODIES. WE GET SICK.

Stagnation in water leads to pollution and bacterial growth. Stagnation in our bodies breaks us down in less visible ways, but you can still feel it happening. We get a new muscle ache or a tweak in our neck we can't shake.

In fact, the definition of stagnation is not flowing or moving. It is also a lack of growth, activity, or development. How can we expect to develop, grow, and thrive if we don't even set aside time to move our bodies? If we don't prioritize moving every single day?

The opposite of stagnation is growth. By taking action and committing to moving each day, you are growing a little stronger, healthier, and a bit more energized each day.

Don't wait to get into action and movement. The longer you wait, the harder it is to get going.

THE IMPORTANCE OF PHYSICAL THERAPY: PREHAB, REHAB AND INJURY PREVENTION

One form of movement I am very passionate about is something I share briefly in the section on self-care and building your chronic pain team. And that is physical therapy.

There are many forms of physical therapy. I think that having a combination of prehab and rehab is key. Prehab is having an exercise or movement routine of things you need to do to keep your body nimble. It allows you to prevent new injuries. It keeps old injuries happy while reducing your pain levels naturally.

Too many people go to physical therapy and treat it the same way they would going to the doctor and asking for a prescription to mask the pain. They don't really want to heal the injury. Instead, they want to get rid of the pain. They want a quick fix.

Real healing is never a quick fix. It requires time, patience, and curiosity, along with commitment.

Find the movements that you need to do daily, weekly, and monthly to keep your body happy and healthy. Once you do have an injury, it's important to work with a physical therapist to rehabilitate it. The goal is to get things back to full motion and mobility.

Take your time finding the right physical therapist for you. If they are only doing manual therapy (i.e., massage, dry needling, or stretching), keep looking. They should be helping you by providing you with strengthening exercises, movements, and stretches to release tight areas or restrictions in your body. To reach full rehabilitation takes time. Work the program. Stick to it.

I know from personal experience, it works. I have rehabilitated from my spinal fusion, knee injuries, a bicep injury, a broken foot, twisted ankles, whiplash, and countless other injuries. Some are small and easy fixes. Others are something I work on daily and will continue for the rest of my life.

But it's worth it because I am not limited. I can still live my life. I have less pain. And that, my friend, is priceless.

MOVEMENT MODIFICATIONS

One common excuse I hear about movement is when people have limitations. Limitations are no excuse to avoid movement. If we allow our limitations to keep us from all forms of movement, we are dooming ourselves to further limitations.

I recently had a problem with my hip. Out of nowhere, I started having tremendous pain in my hip and the muscles around it. I visited my physical therapist to get ideas about what was happening. She gave me some strengthening exercises to work on and some stretches. She also included some joint mobilization movements to incorporate into my daily routine.

While I had to give up running for a couple of weeks, I didn't give up on movement altogether. I swam more instead. I had to avoid certain strokes in the pool, but I was still moving. I also had to avoid certain weightlifting movements. But I didn't give up that routine altogether. I made modifications. I added those new muscle groups into my weight routine to fix my muscle imbalances.

When teaching yoga, I made modifications to increase my hip flexibility. I added some of my physical therapy movements to help my students prevent injuries in their bodies.

Instead of looking at my injury as a limitation, I found ways to modify my movements. I chose to learn and expand my menu of movement options to ones that worked for me while healing the injury.

Next time you have an injury or find yourself with a new limitation, try looking at it as an opportunity to get creative. Look at it as a challenge. How can you move in new ways? What things can you still do? What new things do you need to add to your daily routine to heal yourself?

Find modifications that work for you. If you have no idea where to start, find a physical therapist to work with. Search for "hip prehab" or "hip mobility" on Instagram or YouTube for videos and things you can try and experiment with. That applies to any injury you are working on.

I have worked through shoulder injuries, bicep injuries, joint injuries, broken bones, strains, sprains, and major falls. It is possible to fully heal. And you don't have to give up all movement. You will heal faster and better if you keep moving. Just make the modifications you need to heal.

STILL FEELING RESISTANT TO MOVEMENT?

I hear that. Trying anything new is scary. It can feel really big at first. It can even feel overwhelming. You might not be sure of where to start or if starting even makes sense.

Here's the thing.

WHAT WE FEEL THE MOST RESISTANCE TO DOING IS WHAT WE NEED THE MOST.

Yes, you heard that right. If you are feeling a lot of resistance to adding movement to your life, it means you desperately need it.

So, start today. Get off the couch. Get out of your comfort zone. Take action. Today!

Here are some ways to break through your resistance:

IDEA 1—COMMIT

Choose your top three favorite ways to move.

Of those three, which one is most exciting to you? Write it down.

Commit to doing that movement for fifteen minutes a day for three weeks.

Schedule it in your calendar. Make it a priority. Tell your familyand friends what you are committed to.

Find an accountability partner. Better yet, find someone to do the activity with you for three weeks.

IDEA 2—SET SMALL ACHIEVABLE GOALS

If fifteen minutes a day is too much, start with five minutes a day for the first week. Then bump it up to ten minutes a day the second week and fifteen the week after.

The key is to make movement a habit to start enjoying it again.

On average it takes sixty-six days to create a new habit. Commit to a small goal and stick with it.

It could be as simple as setting your alarm to music you love and waking up each morning and dancing to that song until it's finished. Do that every day for one week.

Then expand your dance party to a five-minute dance party at lunchtime. Make progress that you can build on slowly over time.

Baby steps. Change only requires that we take small steps in the right direction.

IDEA 3—MOVEMENT VISUALIZATION

Visualize yourself doing your favorite activity or movement.

For example, if you love running. Visualize yourself putting on your running shoes and clothes. Putting your earbuds in your ears. What are you listening to?

As you walk outside, what does it smell like? What does the fresh air feel like on your skin? Really dig into all your senses as you visualize this run.

As you visualize your entire run through all your senses, how do you feel? Does it feel good? Do you feel energized? Inspired?

Try visualizing your favorite activity for ten minutes a day every day for a week. You should begin to feel less resistance to that activity.

Also, when we visualize exercise, science has shown that we get some of the same biological benefits as when we actually do that activity. That is a great first step to breaking resistance toward movement.

This is a tool that Olympic athletes use. It works. Give it a try. Let me know how it goes.

And for those of us who are more limited, it's a great way to get the benefits of movement when we can't move.

IDEA 4—BUILD YOUR MOVEMENT MENU

Build a list of every type of movement you enjoy doing. Print it. Post it around the house. Share it with your family and friends. Use it to choose a movement activity to use every day. Make it a family activity. You can choose a movement activity to do together every evening for thirty minutes.

That will allow you to build new traditions and healthy habits as a family. It will build more connection, fun, and energy in your home.

Let me know what your favorite movements are. What does your family love doing together most?

IDEA 5—FIND YOUR INNER CHILD AGAIN

Making change is a lot easier when we make it fun.

Go back to when you were a kid. What did you love doing? Playing tag or dodgeball? Did you play hide and seek and chase each other in the backyard? Was it swinging on a swing set? Was it swimming at the pool and playing silly games with friends like Marco, Polo, or pretending you were on a synchronized swim team?

Whatever it was, no matter how silly, try it. It is *so much fun*! Trust me; I've done this.

When Ian, my boyfriend, and I traveled to Costa Rica, our hotel had this beautiful pool. We spent a lot of time relaxing and reading. But when we got in the pool, we played. We did handstands. We did somersaults. We did flips in the water. I did synchronized swimming while Ian laughed at my movements. It was a *blast*! And a great workout. We had so much fun connecting as the inner kid in each of us.

How can you build more time for play in your life?

Do that. I guarantee it will break through any resistance you have regarding movement. Then you will crave movement instead of dreading it.

MAKE IT HAPPEN

No matter where you are today, you can always use more movement. Movement is what allows you to get into action. You may even find that moving your body will enable you to move in other parts of your life.

When we ignore our physical needs, it bleeds into other parts of our lives.

When you honor our body, you thrive in every part of your life. I guarantee, if you make movement a priority, it will open doors you never knew existed. You will make new friends. You will feel more empowered.

You will have more self-confidence in your appearance and abilities. You will be happier, sleep better, and have less pain.

When you move and take action, you remove any limits you placed on your life. It's the building block to success. So, what's stopping you?

Make it happen. Commit to one tiny step. Move your body.

You've got this!

9

THE IMPORTANCE OF
HOW AND WHAT YOU EAT

"When diet is wrong, medicine is of no use.
When diet is correct, medicine is of no need."

~ AYURVEDIC PROVERB

I'm not a big fan of diets. But I do believe that what we eat matters. And *how* we eat matters even more. Just like anything else we approach for ourselves, this too requires curiosity and experimentation.

I cannot tell you what your body needs. What diet you should be on. You need to find what works best for your body—what feels best for you. No one else can tell you exactly the right mixture of foods for the best version of you. That takes time and patience.

I was gluten, dairy, soy, and sugar-free for eight years. I went gluten-free after reading more about wheat and its effects on inflammation in the body.

I read the book *Grain Brain* and was convinced it was wreaking havoc on my body. Turns out, I was right; I had a severe gluten intolerance, which wasn't surprising as my dad has celiac disease.

I also went dairy-free to help with inflammation but mostly to help my allergies. At the time, I had severe allergies and read a lot about how dairy can make your allergies much worse. So, I gave up dairy, and it seemed to help.

It turns out my stomach was a lot happier without dairy in my diet. I had less gas and less bloating. Win-Win!

I went soy- and sugar-free when I was diagnosed with endometriosis. I began having severe pain with my periods. It was debilitating during my cycle. I could not treat my endometriosis in traditional ways through hormones and birth control. Those treatments gave me migraines and made me really sick. So, I researched all the natural ways to treat endometriosis, including diet. Sugar and soy produce estrogen in the body. And estrogen is what allows the disease to grow.

I also read about how sugar has become a poison, how it's added to nearly every processed food, and how it's creating more diabetics and more inflammatory diseases in our world. That convinced me that it was worth giving up. I still eat fruit in natural form but avoid all other forms of sugar.

If you decide to give up sugar, check out my seven solutions to sugar cravings: https://coachhollyjackson.activehosted.com/f/50 It will help you kick your sugar habit.

When I had my concussion, I changed my diet as well. I naturally began to crave foods like avocado, fatty fish, eggs, and blueberries. Those are foods rich with ingredients that help brain health and brain healing. It's amazing how wise the body is; if only we would stop and listen. Much of what ails us, we can heal naturally. We can fix our diet, our lifestyle and reduce our stress levels.

WHAT YOU EAT

I encourage you to get hyper-curious about your diet. What foods and beverages make you feel the most energized? Which ones make you feel the worst (i.e., bloated, tired, inflamed)?

Experiment with protein forms. Does animal protein or vegetable protein make you feel better? Which animal proteins? Which vegetable proteins? Finding the best form of fuel for your body is essential.

Need Help?

Try out my four-day energy experiment: https://coachhollyjackson.activehosted.com/f/46

For a more detailed explanation of how to use this tool, consider joining the Health Secrets Master Class today: https://hollyjeanjackson.com/healthsecrets

ELIMINATION DIETS

If you discover a food that is bothering you, consider eliminating it from your diet. Keep a journal to track how you feel after eliminating it. When you have no idea which foods are bothering you, it can be helpful to do an elimination diet. There are many guides online. You can work with a doctor or a nutritionist to design one for you and your needs.

After you design a baseline with some basic foods, you'll begin adding one food back at a time. You'll carefully track how you feel as you add foods back in. If one bothers you, that's great news because you've identified a problem with food. I have done many elimination diets. I want to share my ninja tips based on my experiences.

ELIMINATION DIET DOS AND DON'TS:

- Work with a professional you trust.
- Do your research.
- Try adding supplements to the mix.
- Find easy to go solutions that work with your new diet.
- Get creative and have fun with it.
- Try new recipes.

- Find a therapist or life coach to work with for the emotional impacts.
- Don't pick a diet that is too limited. Find one that's robust and manageable.
- Don't obsess. Do your best, but don't let it ruin the moment.
- Don't stick with it for too long. Revisit it from time to time. Try adding foods back in. The gut can heal over time.
- Don't stop trying new things.

Whatever diet you land on, try not to think of it as a diet. Think of it as finding the best fuel for your body, taking care of yourself, and taking control of your healing journey.

Remember, it's a journey. The journey is always ebbing and flowing. Go with the flow and have fun.

EMOTIONAL SUPPORT

When you change your diet, it has emotional impacts as well. Sometimes those around you will find it to be frustrating. They may not be very supportive.

I remember when I went gluten- and dairy-free, I lost some friendships. Upon reflection, they weren't very good friends. Real friends support each other no matter what, especially when it comes to our health.

I had many friends that gave up trying to find places to eat with me. They just asked me to choose places to eat. That is fair, though. They don't know everything about what we need. But it does mean it takes more research on our end to make sure we have options for where to eat.

I had one close friend at the time who got really angry with me about my dietary restrictions. We went on a trip together to Lake Tahoe to go cycling and stayed with a friend of hers. We went out to lunch one afternoon. I asked the waiter, "What options do you have that are gluten and dairy free?" The waiter was sweet and helpful.

Later that day, Sally pulled me aside and told me, "Holly I'm so embarrassed by you. My friend has been nice enough to let us stay with him. And here you are making a big deal out of your diet. That's really not cool. I don't appreciate it. Please stop making such a scene." I was dumbfounded. I started crying. *How on earth could someone I considered to be such a dear friend have so little compassion?*

We had a long conversation about this but ultimately this was the end of that friendship. Deep down, I could never be friends with someone who had such little compassion for something that was important to my health and wellbeing.

Real friends will be supportive of the changes you make. They'll ask you what you can and can't eat when they have you over for dinner. They'll work with you on social situations when food is involved. Find your real friends and distance yourself from those who don't support you, especially when it comes to your health.

I will never forget, a dear friend of mine, Sanketh, invited me over for lunch. He texted me asking, "What are your dietary restrictions again?" I wrote back, "You don't need to worry. I can bring my own lunch." He said, "Nonsense, I want to cook for you!" When I came over for lunch, he asked me, "How is your new diet going? Is it helping your health? What do the doctors say?" He genuinely cared about me and my health. He didn't see my diet as a burden because he cared about me.

I find that when we're faced with significant lifestyle changes, that's when we discover who our real friends are. The ones who are curious and supportive are true diamonds in the rough. The ones who seem annoyed, impatient, or frustrated, are the ones you need to let go. You have outgrown them and they aren't serving you anymore.

Not being able to eat many things can make social interactions less than fun. It can feel frustrating, depressing, limiting, and daunting. There may be times when you can't find anything to eat. Or times when loved ones are eating some of your favorite foods that you can no longer eat.

Make sure you put together a plan to support yourself emotionally as you change what you eat. As we'll explore in this next section, how we are when we eat is just as important. If you're feeling stressed from your diet, it'll impact the nutritional value you get from what you eat.

Boost your self-care routine to help support yourself.

HOW YOU EAT

Just as important as what we eat is *how* we eat. If you're stressed out and you go to eat a meal, do you think that's good for you? It's important that we check in with how we feel before we eat.

Too often, people will tune out and watch television while they eat. Then they wonder how they ate so much. They're so out of tune with what their bodies need that they overeat. You cannot listen to your body if you're zoned out.

CHECK IN

Before you start a meal, try checking in with yourself first. See how you're feeling. If you're stressed or feeling off, take one or two minutes to get your mind right first. Do a short meditation or visualization. Or simply stop and breathe deeply. It only takes one minute to reset your nervous system—only one minute to get to a peaceful state of being. You're worth it. Take the minute to get into a good state of being. That way, your food will be more nourishing.

VISUALIZATION AND FOOD

Sometimes I find myself in situations when there are no good food options for me to eat. Perhaps there is dairy in the airplane food, and I could not bring my own. If that is the case, I like to visualize that I'm eating the most nourishing and healthy food for my body. I visualize it healing my cells, repairing my body, and nourishing my system.

It sounds silly, but it works. When I don't do that and have to eat less than ideal food, I always feel worse. That is not to say eat whatever you want, even if it's bad for your body. It is to say, when faced with less-than-ideal situations, the mind is very powerful.

How you show up when you eat has a *huge* impact on you.

DO NOTHING BUT EAT

Another way to improve nourishment from a meal is to do nothing but enjoy your meal. Don't watch TV, play on your phone, or even read a book. Enjoy your meal. Imagine all that went into bringing you that food. The farmers who grew and harvested the ingredients. The animals who gave life to nourish us. The chef who prepared it. Enjoy every single bite with delight. Enjoy the flavor, the colors, the texture, every aspect of each bite you take. Make your meal a sensory experience. I guarantee you'll enjoy your food much more when you eat that way.

THE TWENTY-MINUTE MEAL

Too many of us rush through our meal. We look at it as a means to an end. We don't stop and enjoy our food. We eat our meals stressed out and rushed. And we wonder why we gain weight. Why do we feel awful after eating? Why do we feel full or bloated?

It takes the brain and body twenty minutes to process if it's full. That means if you're eating your meal faster than twenty minutes, you'll never feel full.

THE TWENTY-MINUTE MEAL GUIDE CHALLENGE:
https://coachhollyjackson.activehosted.com/f/48

- Eat your meal as you normally would and time it.
- Write down how many minutes it takes you to eat.
- For your next meal, try to eat a bit slower. Put your fork down between bites. Have a sip of water. Be sure to time your meal.
- With each meal, try making it last five minutes longer until you get to twenty minutes.
- Try to eat every meal in twenty minutes. No faster. Slower is okay. For the best nourishment from our food, it is important that we take our time.

That allows the body and brain to determine when it's full. Any meal eaten faster than that and you won't know if you're full. You'll likely eat too much. When you do feel full, try pushing your plate away to signal you're done. Try stating out loud that your meal is complete. Finding a way to signal you're done can be helpful. What and how you eat matters. I challenge you to find the best foods and ways to eat that bring you the most nourishment and healing. I guarantee you'll feel better.

You can even do these challenges with your family. Make it a family experiment. Have fun with it!

10

COPING WITH CHRONIC PAIN

"I thank God for my handicaps, for, through the,
I have found myself, my work, and my God."

~HELEN KELLER

Have you ever found yourself in so much pain that you're praying out to God to make it go away—to give you one moment without suffering?

That is what it feels like when you're in severe pain. Imagine that gripping pain lasting for days, then months, then years, and even decades. It's hard to fathom.

And yet, one in five adults in the US experiences chronic pain and 8% have high-impact chronic pain.
(reference: https://www.cdc.gov/mmwr/volumes/67/wr/mm6736a2.htm)

Chronic pain is debilitating—mentally, physically, emotionally, and spiritually. If you don't have the right tools to combat it, it can leave you in shambles. A shell of who you once were. It's easy to lose your identity to chronic pain. Believe me; I've been there.

While this next story is one we have already covered, we will take a much deeper dive here. There are many nuggets of wisdom for how to navigate any chronic pain challenge you are facing today.

In my teens, I suffered from back pain on and off. I worked with a chiropractor for years. It helped some, but over time, as I hit my early twenties, I began having more severe pain.

Then I had a car accident on my way to work one morning. A utility van came out of nowhere and ran a red light. I t-boned into the van at sixty miles per hour. It was terrifying. My airbag didn't deploy, which in hindsight may have been a blessing. It would have made my injuries worse.

I didn't go to the hospital. I was in so much shock that I didn't have pain right away. But over time, I began having severe pain. My lower back sent a shooting pain down my legs. My pain went from somewhat manageable to debilitating. I would be standing, and then all of a sudden, I would feel crippling pain. All kinds of movement would create pain. It was hard to avoid.

I began working with pain specialists. I tried everything—physical therapy, cortisone injections, chiropractic care, etc. You name it; I tried it.

I even did epidural injections in my spine. And here you were thinking these were only for women in labor; me too. I did three rounds of injections. They were intense. They would find the pain point area and intentionally inject fluid into it to see if they had the right trigger point. I couldn't move while they did it. It felt like the pain I had already experienced times a million.

I wanted to scream or die. It was so bad. I could feel the ringing in my ears. My body felt like it was on fire. Then they would add the cortisol to help calm the area—relief at last. So much relief sometimes I would find myself passing out—losing touch with reality due to the relief from such intense pain. The last round of epidural injections seemed to help my lower back pain. But I still had a lot of chronic pain throughout my neck and spine.

Then one day, I found a specialist who worked with people with spinal challenges—the Hey Clinic. I set up an appointment with Dr. Hey. He told me, "You have a seventy-two-degree curve in your spine and a slight scoliosis curve." A scoliosis curve is a curve side to side or left to right. My seventy-two-degree curve was kyphotic (i.e., curving forward).

He explained that "This degeneration of your spine is likely genetic. There's nothing that you did wrong." That was a relief as I had been ridiculed by my parents and husband for years, telling me I'd had bad posture.

He told me, "If you don't correct the curve, it will likely increase, and you could go into organ failure if that happens. If left uncorrected, getting pregnant, gaining weight, and life, in general, could cause your spine to degrade further."

Ultimately, I needed surgery to correct ten levels of my spine that were severely degraded. That degradation was what had been causing my shooting nerve pain and chronic pain for years. I was relieved. Finally, I had answers. I wasn't crazy. My pain was real. It wasn't in my head. After seeing expert after expert, I finally knew what was wrong, and I knew how to fix it!

When you have chronic pain, it's very lonely. It makes you feel crazy because no one else can feel what you feel. And even though you may appear to be healthy on the outside, you're reeling on the inside. Your pain is the center of your world because it's so consuming. But life goes on for those around you. They can't understand why pain has stolen your attention. Why pain has changed who you are. Why you can't get back to who you were before.

I scheduled my surgery for two months later. During surgery, they had to break my spine in ten places where it was forming a bad curvature. Then they took two titanium rods and drilled screws into my spine to correct the curve to thirty degrees.

When I woke up, the pain was excruciating. It felt like I had rods in my spine because I did. And while that may sound silly, it felt really invasive.

The pain was intense. I was on morphine and other medications for three to five days in the hospital. I was hospitalized for five days. Some nights, the pain was so bad, even with the drugs, I would hold my husband's hand and beg God for mercy.

When I got home, it wasn't much better. My mom came and took care of me for the first week as my husband had to go back to working in another state. She forced me to do small things each day that weren't centered around me or my pain. That was some of the best advice I would get early on.

Don't cave into the pain. Make space for other things and people.

After the first week at home, I was on my own. I had our dog, Rocky, to take care of. Luckily, he seemed to understand intuitively that I was in pain. He never tried to jump on me or pull me on his leash. He was protective of me, even more so than before.

I had quite a few limitations. I couldn't lift anything heavier than a gallon of milk for months. I couldn't turn my neck or bend my spine for six months. Doing life on your own with those constraints forced me to get creative.

The pain was relentless. I didn't have the nerve pain I'd had before. But I was faced with intense muscular pain. My body was not adjusting well to the new shape of my spine. It was fighting back and gripping.

I was prescribed muscle relaxants and painkillers. It took me six months to get off the painkillers and another three to four years to recognize that I was addicted to the muscle relaxants, and I got off of them.

THE TURNING POINT

One day I was talking to my best friend, Martina. It was a few years after my surgery. I was telling her about my pain yet again.

She stopped me. "Holly, I love you. I can't imagine what it's like to be experiencing the pain you're in. But I can't stand by and not say anything. The Holly I knew is gone. I don't even recognize who you are today. You're so consumed by your pain; it's literally the only thing you talk about. And I can't stand it. I can't stand by and lose my best friend. So, until you get back to you, I can't talk to you. I can't be your friend. I'm so sorry."

Woah!

My immediate reaction was outrage and disbelief. How could my best friend judge me that way? How could she not understand my pain? It was so unfair.

But then I sat with it over the next several days. I realized she was right. I also realized that it took a tremendous amount of courage for her to be so honest with me—to be so vulnerable and possibly lose our friendship forever.

I suddenly felt incredibly grateful that I had such an amazing friend—someone who loved me so much that they would risk losing it all for me—that they loved me enough to call me on my own shit.

If you get nothing from this book, I hope you hear this . . .

Surround yourself with people who love you so much that they call you on your shit. They tell you when you're out of line, off track, or being ridiculous.

The people who don't speak up don't care enough. It takes love and courage to be vulnerable and brutally honest.

WHAT WE NEED TO HEAL IS *BRUTAL HONESTY*

Healing is an inside job. But it takes loved ones around us acting as a mirror to help us see our blind spots, to help us shift our perspective, to help us get back on track. I'd lost my identity altogether to my pain. And it took my dear friend calling me on it to help me wake up.

That was my turning point.

After it settled in, I started working on healing from the inside. I found a cognitive behavioral therapist to help me shift my thinking, to help me rewire my brain and habits.

I started reading about how to heal from chronic pain. I started to find things to focus on that I was grateful for that had nothing to do with my pain. I reached out to friends to ask them about their lives. I began to discover that being present with loved ones and hearing about their lives was healing. It helped me focus on something other than my pain, other than myself. And helping loved ones helped even more.

If you're experiencing chronic pain today, one of the most healing things is doing something for someone else. The feeling you get from helping others is healing. That is not me diminishing your pain. But I do want to show you that you can live with your pain without losing yourself.

But it's a choice. A choice you make every single second of every day. There are still moments in my life when pain wins. *But* now, I have tools and community that help me get back on track much faster. And I don't lose myself to pain for very long.

LABELS: DON'T PUT YOURSELF IN A BOX

Shortly after my surgery, I was given the option to list myself as disabled. The nursing team came to me and said, "Here is all the information on disability benefits. You qualify and should apply. You can also have a permanent handicap placard if you apply. For now, you will have a placard for the first six months of your recovery. What questions can we answer for you?"

My mind was racing. *What do you mean I'm disabled? Disabled for life? I will need a handicap placard forever? I thought this surgery was meant to heal me and not put limitations on me. Isn't labeling myself disabled a significant limitation?*

I asked, "Why would I apply for disability? I thought the surgeon told me I would live a normal, full life?" The nurse replied, "This is the standard procedure. You have a significant setback that warrants disability. If you'd like to apply you can. You aren't required to. But there's nothing wrong with being disabled either."

Luckily, when offered the option, I was already working with a therapist and surrounded by loved ones who had my back. Otherwise, I might have chosen to use that label.

For me, opting in for disability would have affected my mental state too much. I feared I would lose my identity to disability. I didn't want a label to create a glass ceiling. I didn't want to be looked at differently.

I was young. When faced with that option, it felt like my life was coming to an end. Signing that application would mean giving up on adventure. It would mean I couldn't skydive, backpack, cycle, travel, weight lift, do yoga, and much more.

It took me years to prove my surgeons and countless doctors wrong— that I could live a full and normal life. I've had to train new doctors not to question my surgery but to support me in moving forward. The words we use and hear from others have great power. Listen to them carefully, and use them.

Again, this was how I felt *personally*.

That is *not* to say that being listed as disabled is a bad thing. If you have a disability and need the support, that is exactly what it's there for. I just want to warn you; don't let it impact your mindset. That is the danger with any label. It simplifies complex issues. Pain is complex, and there are ways to navigate.

There will be seasons when it feels like the pain is all-consuming. And then there are seasons when you'll feel like a superhero, capable of doing anything because you've worked hard on healing. Whatever you choose, don't put yourself in a box. Don't allow a label to corner you. Anything is possible. Healing is an inside job. And the mind is the most powerful asset we have.

You can do this!

NAVIGATING CHRONIC PAIN, YOUR ROADMAP

I hope you feel empowered and ready to transform your pain, to heal from the inside. I recommend taking this section one step at a time. Work through each step at your own pace. Move to the next step when you're ready. And if you get stuck or backslide, go back to step one. Be patient and kind to yourself.

Remember to enjoy the journey. And don't forget to celebrate your progress, even the smallest of steps.

Here is your roadmap to transforming your pain:

- Step One: Acceptance
- Step Two: Curiosity
- Step Three: Research and Advocate for Your Best Care
- Step Four: Mindset, Mindset, Mindset!
- Step Five: Build a Community
- Step Six: Build Your Toolkit and Use It
- Step Seven: Help Others. Pay it Forward

Let's dive into these one at a time, step by step.

Download your copy of the Chronic Pain Roadmap at https://coachhollyjackson.activehosted.com/f/60

STEP ONE: ACCEPTANCE

One of the most depleting things we can do is resist reality. When we try to deny that a loved one has died, denying our pain, it only hurts us more. It keeps us trapped, unable to move forward.

The first step to healing anything is acceptance. Acceptance is *not* the same thing as a victim mindset. Nor is it the same thing as limiting yourself.

I want to be clear. Acceptance means you aren't resisting what's happening. It means you aren't denying how you feel. It means you're giving space to and acknowledging what's happening in your body and your life.

Acceptance can be painful. The mind uses denial to protect us. When we deny things, we don't have to deal with them. It's a coping mechanism, but it only works in the short term. Eventually, denial can become depleting and reckless.

If you've been dealing with chronic pain, it's time to accept it. Accept your injury, ailment, disease, or sickness. Whatever it is, don't deny that it's part of your reality. When we acknowledge our pain, we can begin learning how to work with it, how to learn from it, and how to use tools to shift it. The longer we deny it, the easier it will be for us to fall victim to it and become consumed by it. Don't become a victim of your pain.

Acknowledge and accept it and move on to step two.

STEP TWO: CURIOSITY

Instead of judging your pain, try looking at it from a new perspective. Consider getting curious about your pain. What does your pain say about your emotional wellbeing? Is there anything you're holding onto there? Is there anything you could heal?

What does your pain say about your spiritual well-being? Is it trying to get you to look at something new? To be more open? To consider new possibilities?

The biggest challenge I hear from clients and loved ones facing chronic pain is asking why? Why me? It's a heavy and loaded question, and it doesn't lead to anything helpful. You can try to find the silver lining, and that's a wonderful approach. But it keeps you focused on the pain.

We're trying to find ways to shift into new possibilities—where our lives are full of many things, and pain is one component of that. Beyond doing the internal work that is often necessary for healing, I encourage you to explore all your options for healing. That includes non-traditional medicine and services.

Research and explore all the possibilities to help your pain. Keep an open mind. Start experimenting with what works best for you and your body.

Here are some ideas to consider exploring:

- Acupuncture
- Energy healing (reiki)
- Spiritual healing (a shaman)
- Essential oils
- Vitamins and supplements
- Anti-inflammatory diets and working with a nutritionist
- Functional medicine
- Chiropractic
- Sensory deprivation tank floats
- Yoga
- Breath work (ecstatic breathing, fire breathing, etc.)
- Ecstatic dance
- Bioidentical hormones
- Sound healing (sound bowels, etc.)
- Homeopathic treatments
- Osteopathic adjustments
- Therapy or counseling
- Life coaching
- Health coaching
- Meditation
- Affirmation work
- Chanting

- Drum circles
- CBD oils
- Chinese herbs

The list is endless. There are new discoveries coming out every day. There are old sciences and practices that span hundreds of years. There is wisdom in that as well.

Get empowered. Be excited. Find the healing modalities that work best for you. It takes time, so don't get frustrated. If something doesn't work, great! You've ruled that out. Move on to the next thing.

But also, it can take some time for something new to work. Nutrition work and using supplements takes months before you see an impact. Floating takes at least a month of consistent floating to see a marked difference. Be patient and remain open and hopeful.

If something works for you, be sure to share it with a loved one if they need support or are experiencing pain. But realize that what works for you may not work for them. Never try to push or force anything on someone else.

It's all a very personal and grand experiment. Have fun with it and share!

STEP THREE: RESEARCH AND ADVOCATE FOR YOUR BEST CARE

Now that you're more aware of what works for you, it's important to build your care team. In addition to the non-traditional support you need, you want to find your care team. It's important that you research and find the best doctors for you—the ones who support you, who are open to non-traditional ideas, and who respect your boundaries.

Depending on your chronic pain, your core care team will vary. It will take time to figure out who you need to see regularly. Once you do, you know they're on your team.

My Core Care Team Includes:

- Chiropractor
- Physical therapist
- Float center
- Life coach

- Energy coach
- Business coach
- Doctor
- OBGYN
- Neurologist
- Massage therapist

It seems like a lot, doesn't it? But that is the sweet spot for me. For me to manage my spinal fusion pain and other health challenges, I must interact with my core team.

I found that my sweet spot for chiropractic and PT is once every three to six weeks, depending on my stress levels and activities. I float twice a month. I see my coaches once every four to eight weeks. I get a massage every four weeks. And I see my doctors as needed.

And guess what? It's 100% worth it.

I am able to do things I never thought I would be able to. My partner and I are talking about having a child. In the past, I never thought my body could handle being a mom. I didn't think I could carry a child.

Now, I have my team of healers. I know what I need to do on my own to manage my health—who I need to see when something flares up. That took me years to fine-tune. That's not to say I didn't improve over time. I did. But I also had setbacks along the way. Don't let missteps and setbacks discourage you. Progress is progress, and missteps are something we can learn from.

You may be wondering, how do I select the right people for my health team? Great question!

HERE ARE SOME CRITERIA TO CONSIDER:

- They have great reviews online
- They don't rush you, and they listen carefully
- They're open-minded
- They don't jump to negative labels, conclusions, or make defeating comments about your health

- You can tell and feel that they care when you see them
- They feel like they're partnering with you on your health (they listen to your ideas and research them)
- When you give them feedback, they hear it and take action on it

It is so important. You want your care team to be partners. You want them to be invested in your health and wellbeing. That means you're always an avid student, trying to learn more about improving your health and wellbeing. You share with your team the new ideas, research, and experiments you have uncovered. It also means that when they say something that doesn't sit well with you, you speak up and share.

I will never forget the time I researched and found an amazing doctor who specialized in internal medicine, had homeopathic experience and was an osteopath. I was so excited to meet him. Within the first few minutes of meeting him and sharing my health history, he said, "Why on earth did you fuse ten levels of your spine? That was a terrible decision." I looked at him and said as calmly as I was able to, "You'll never say anything like that to me again if we're going to work together. What's done is done. It doesn't help my healing to hear you tell me you think it was a terrible idea. I can't go back in time. I'm here to find someone to help me heal and grow. If that's not you, tell me now, so we don't waste any time."

Guess what? He heard me. He apologized. We had a great session, and he ended up being my doctor for twelve years. The only reason we stopped working together was that I moved out of state.

To build that partnership, you have to be willing to speak up for yourself. You have to be honest and vulnerable. And if they don't respond well, move on to a new doctor. They aren't the right fit for you. It does take time to find the right person with the right chemistry and expertise for you.

You've got this!

STEP FOUR: MINDSET, MINDSET, MINDSET!

One of the biggest challenges I faced when shifting my chronic pain was my mindset. When I began listening to my thoughts, they were all very negative. I had streams of thoughts of being a victim. Lots of angry thoughts.

This is what my mind sounded like back then.

"You'll never live a normal life. Having a family is out of the question. No one wants to be around you. You're miserable. You'll never summit that mountain on your bucket list. You'll never accomplish your dreams or goals. Your pain will never go away. You're doomed to live like this forever . . . alone. You might as well give up now."

Wow! How incredibly depressing.

How on earth can we heal our bodies if these are the toxic thoughts we're telling ourselves? The reality is, you can't heal until you get your mind straight.

So how do you begin to work on your mindset? The first step is awareness. Start paying attention to what you're thinking throughout the day. Sit with your journal every morning and night to tune in. Tune in with curiosity, not judgment. Then write down everything that came up. Start bucketing your thoughts into different sections. For example, which thoughts are about being a victim and which ones are about anger.

The next step is to identify the core beliefs that are driving those thought patterns. The bucketing exercise above will help you begin to identify them. As discussed in chapter seven, you can use those activities and exercises to help shift the mindset tied to your pain as well.

Some specific things to watch out for related to chronic pain are as follows:

- Don't let pain become the center of your life or thoughts
- Don't let your disability define or label you
- Don't believe there is something wrong with you
- Don't believe negative things a doctor or someone in a white coat shares with you. Research it first. Stand up for yourself.

It's easy to let your pain consume your thoughts. It takes a lot of work, determination, commitment, and courage to face your pain and shift into something healthier.

The final step after using all the tools from chapter seven is to be grateful. Be grateful for who you are, including your pain, your disease, your "fill in the blank." Without those ailments or circumstances, you wouldn't be who you are today.

This is a difficult step. It's similar to forgiveness. It's something you work on every day, every single moment. It's a choice.

YOU CAN CHOOSE YOUR PAIN, OR YOU CAN CHOOSE GRATITUDE.

Even when you have a flare-up, a setback, or incredible pain, choose gratitude and joy. Choose to shift into focusing on something else. There is so much more to life than our pain. Step into that.

STEP FIVE: BUILD A COMMUNITY

Support and community are essential to being human. And chronic pain can feel very lonely. It can be very isolating. That is why it's essential for you to build a community.

When I went through my divorce, I knew that part of my contribution to the marriage ending was my codependency. So, I joined a group called Celebrate Recovery. It's a community of others who also face challenges, addictions, and pain who want to shift it.

That community was transformational for me. It provided me with a safe container to share my pain, to explore what I needed to work on without judgment, and to feel all my emotions without shame. I was able to be raw, vulnerable, and I didn't have to wear a mask or sugarcoat anything. It was so freeing.

While that community was more focused on shifting addiction or changing a behavior, as we have discussed, healing is an inner game. Any group you can find that will help you shift your emotional pain benefits your healing.

Find support groups that work for you. They have groups all around the world for individuals with cancer, with various diseases, for chronic pain, and there are loads of groups for emotional hurts as well. Research what's available in your community. Find a few you want to explore. Check them out. Don't let your fear get in the way here. Take action on this step. Don't get stuck. Tell a loved one your plan to attend three groups and on what day for accountability.

It can be very scary to join a support group. But anything worth doing is always a little scary. And it is so worthwhile. I can't tell you how important community has been for my healing and growth. I am a member of several communities. I joined a church for a few years after my divorce. It was pivotal in providing me with support and community during a difficult transition. I became part of the team that taught for the children's ministry. It was incredibly rewarding. It helped me forge new, healthy relationships. It helped me feel safe again.

I am also a swimmer, so I joined the U.S. Masters Swimming team years ago and found a local swim team to join. Wherever I move in the US or while I travel, I can always find a team to swim with. The vibe of my fellow swimmers always lifts me up. No matter where I move, I feel at home.

I love cycling and got into road biking several years ago. I found a community of cyclists while I was living in the Bay Area, and I joined them for cycling adventures. But the reality is that no matter what community I join, they become part of my circle of friends. And some of them become part of my chosen family.

I encourage you to build your community and tribe. Get curious about your hobbies and what you love, and join groups that do those things. It doesn't have to be a group that focuses on pain. It can be a fun art group. It could be a reading club. The goal is to surround yourself with people who support you and people who accept you, including your limitations or boundaries.

And for the people who don't support you, they aren't part of your tribe. Move on. There are so many people out there who can't wait to meet you. Get out there. Build connection, joy, and fun today!

STEP SIX: BUILD YOUR TOOLKIT AND USE IT

In step two, you got curious and explored non-traditional methods to work with your pain. That was from the lens of building your health care team in step three.

Now, we want to build your self-care toolkit. You can also revisit chapter five on self-care for more ideas. That includes any activities, exercises, or services that help you manage your physical pain and stress.

Our goal here is to have a list of tools we can go to anytime we're triggered. Anytime our pain hits an all-time high. Anytime life throws us a stressful curveball. That way, we have a simple list of what we can do. Instead of falling back into a victim mindset, we'll be equipped to take action and get back on track faster.

SOME IDEAS FOR YOUR TOOLKIT:

- Breathwork (straw breathing, counted breathing, long exhales)
- Meditation
- Visualization
- Exercise/movement (run, bike, swim, dance)
- Journaling
- Affirmations
- Tapping into your community(ies)
- Connection (connect with a friend, family, loved one)
- Screaming into a pillow
- Massage
- Mani/pedi or spa day
- Float
- Go on a hike or a walk outside
- Grounding (sit on the grass, garden with your hands in the dirt)
- Hugs or cuddling
- Laughter (watch a funny video, a comedian, or call a funny friend)
- Play the piano (or sing or drum)

Each person's toolkit will be very different. Have fun with this. Explore your favorite hobbies from when you were a kid. Below are some questions to reflect on to start getting ideas for your toolkit.

QUESTIONS TO CONSIDER:

- What activities, people, etc. bring you the most joy?
- What puts you into a state of flow (where you lose track of time)?
- What makes you laugh?
- What cheers you up on your worst day?
- Who always leaves you feeling better no matter what?
- When you're stressed out or anxious, what grounds you (i.e., makes you feel better)?

Individuals with chronic pain are blessed with taking excellent care of their bodies. We're blessed with a heightened awareness of our bodies. Use it. Explore it. Have fun with it. And share it.

STEP SEVEN: HELP OTHERS, PAY IT FORWARD

As soon as you get a quick win, it's important to pass it on. Share it with someone else. Imagine how grateful you would have been if you had those tools years ago, months ago. Why wait to become a master of your pain? Share anything you find useful with someone else who needs it. Not to mention, you'll feel better sharing it. You'll feel gratitude, joy, and a sense of community in sharing. It's what makes us human. We have a need to share—a need to be seen and heard.

USE YOUR GIFTS AND SKILLS TO HELP OTHERS HEAL.

Most chronically challenged people that have survived and thrived through it are innately healers because they have walked it. They use their experience and their challenges to help others. In doing so, they heal themselves even more. We learn by helping others. We grow in community.

Pay it forward. Always.

Need Help?

Download your copy of the Chronic Pain Roadmap at https://coachhollyjackson.activehosted.com/f/60 for a printed reminder of the steps you need to take.

11

OWN YOUR HEALTH JOURNEY

"All the wonders you seek are within yourself."

~SIR THOMAS BROWN

We've covered a lot of ground in this book. You now have the strategies and tools necessary to begin your journey to healing. I hope you're feeling empowered and excited.

To get the most out of this book, I recommend going back and reviewing one chapter at a time. Take action on something. Make forward progress. Celebrate even the smallest of progress.

Set new goals to get to that next level of healing and whole health. And if you're stuck on how to set new goals, check out my goal setting worksheet at https://coachhollyjackson.activehosted.com/f/56

THERE IS ALWAYS A NEXT LEVEL

After my back surgery, I believed I couldn't carry a child—that pregnancy wasn't safe for my body. I also believed after holding my newborn nephew that I could never adopt a newborn child. After holding him for a brief while, my back went out for almost a week. I decided then that I would never be a mother. At least not to an infant.

I didn't want to bring an innocent child into the world and be a terrible mother. I knew that if I carried a child to delivery, my pain level would be so high that I would be short-tempered and irrational. I would not be in the right mindset to be a good mother.

Based on that belief, I chose to get my tubes removed. I knew that I would never have an abortion. But I also knew I didn't want to bring a child into the world under those circumstances. And so, I did it.

About a year ago, I moved back to North Carolina. I surrounded myself with my family and friends. I met an amazing man. He and my physical therapist began to challenge me. They gave me hope.

Ian believed that I could improve my back and neck pain. He believed I could improve my shoulder mobility. He called me on my BS. When I used my spinal fusion as an excuse, and he didn't buy it, he called me out on it. He said, "For this, that's BS. You can do that. Let me show you how."

So, I started putting in the time to do these new exercises. I gave up swimming and cycling for six months. They were adding to my shoulder mobility issue. I needed time to grow new muscles, relax tightened muscles, and create new habits.

I began to see improvements slowly over time. My shoulder mobility is nearly normal now. I don't experience nearly as much pain. I'm able to travel, and I have the tools I need when I do have a flare-up.

After some time, Ian and I had an experience that left us wondering if we wanted to have a biological child. I got my period three weeks late. I went to see my doctor, and he said we should do a pregnancy test.

Dumbfounded, I looked at him and said, "Why on earth would we do that? I don't have tubes. How could I get pregnant?" He said, "Ms. Jackson, crazier things have happened. The first thing we should do is rule out pregnancy. Then we can go from there." When I finally got the test results back, and it said negative, I found myself heartbroken—a little relieved but mostly really sad.

I went to Ian, and we talked about our future. I said, "This whole thing has made it really clear to me that I want to be a mother. That I want to try and have a biological child. And that I want to do that with you. I know we briefly talked about this when we started dating, but I really want to see where you are on this." Ian shared that he felt the same way. He wanted to try and have a child.

We began exploring options for having a child. Yesterday we met with a fertility specialist, and we're pursuing our options to start our family. I share this because I don't want you to ever allow your own beliefs or the beliefs of someone else to limit your possibilities.

I WANT YOU TO REJECT THAT THERE IS A CEILING TO WHAT YOU CAN HEAL.

If someone says it's impossible, you should feel more empowered to prove them wrong. Don't let their defeated view of the world keep you down. Don't let it become your setback.

I'll also share that the fertility appointment was initially pretty depressing, and I did feel defeated. I'm sharing this because even though I have been working this system for decades now, I, too, am human. It doesn't mean we don't have emotions or strong feelings.

You still need to allow yourself the space to process what you feel. But don't stay stuck there. Use the system. Own your healing—advocate for yourself. And do what you need to do to achieve your goals.

Going back to my story, the fertility specialist urged us to start trying IVF therapies immediately. She shared that we have a 30% chance with each cycle to get pregnant. Leaving the appointment, I felt like I had just been hurled up and down an emotional, spiritual roller coaster. I felt exhausted, distraught, depressed, and in loads of fear–fear that we would never have a family.

The doctor said I needed to make sure pregnancy was safe for me. She shared that I have an extremely low egg count. She even stated that my past surgeon may have done something that caused damage to my ovaries. None of these things made me feel optimistic. I felt anger. Anger with my surgeon. Anger with myself for choosing to remove my tubes. Anger about the timing of things in life and the pressure this was placing on Ian and me.

I felt hopeless. I felt like a victim. I started going down the rabbit hole. So, I went home, and I cried. I let myself feel what I was feeling. I sobbed. I screamed into a pillow. And then, I called my mom and my sister.

FIND YOUR PEOPLE

I knew I needed my family. And I knew I needed to talk to women who would understand the emotional roller coaster I was on. They reminded me that statistics are just numbers—that if we really want a child, we'll have a child, that there are lots of options.

My mom reminded me of all the signs of fertility I have had. The visions of having a daughter I have had for years. She reminded me that while building my business, I had doubts. But I remained faithful. I continued to take action. I continued to believe and visualize the future I wanted. And it worked.

She reminded me of how powerful I am. She said, "Go feel what you need to feel. Run, scream, cry, get it out of your system. And then forget about the numbers. Forget what the doctor said. Talk with Ian and figure out what feels best for you two. Take the action you need today. And continue to believe. Have faith. Visualize your future as a mother—your future with your family. You can do anything you want to. Never forget that. Focus on that."

Wow! You see, that is why I dedicated this book to my mother. I call her Yoda. She is so wise. She has struggled with so many health challenges herself. She has so much wisdom and generosity to share with the world. She gets it.

She faced allergies, sinus infections, sinus surgery, and she copes with her disease, Multiple Sclerosis. Yet, she doesn't let it get her down. She lives life fully. She pays it forward. She focuses on her community and on paying it forward.

You may not be blessed with someone in your family who has these qualities. I urge you to find your one or two inner-circle people who can help you get out of your spiral. Those are people who know you, love you, and support you no matter what life throws your way. They'll be real with you but always have your back. They lift you up. They provide wisdom. They let you vent. They offer advice when you ask for it. And then help you get out of your spiral with love and light.

Once you find your people, be sure you're supporting them as well. Ask them how you can hold them accountable. What are their next goals for growth? What are they struggling with? Listen and share any insights you can offer. Healthy relationships are always a two-way street. Make sure you aren't only taking and asking for more. Pay it forward as well.

That's why it's important to have a community beyond your two core inner-circle people. You need a tribe to thrive. You need friends to laugh with. Friends to learn with. Friends to work out with. Friends to vent to. Friends to work with.

I believe we have people who come into our lives for a reason, for a season, and for life. Friends come and go, and some stay for a lifetime.

Explore if someone is in your life for a reason (i.e., to teach you something). Explore if they're in your life for a season (i.e., to help you through a difficult situation or transition). And be grateful when you find those few special souls who are your friends for life. Never take them for granted.

And in case you're wondering, we ended up getting new lab results, which increases our odds of having a family when the timing is right for us. That is the perfect example of advocating for yourself—of not believing it until you get a second and a third opinion—of not believing limitations are real until you've tried every possibility out there.

Don't let doctors in white coats bring you down or hold you back. There is always something else you can try. Someone new you can lean on. If it's something you really want or want to fix, it's possible. Anything you set your mind to is possible.

STAY THE COURSE

You may be wondering how I stay on track? How do I continue to improve and grow?

HERE'S A CHECKLIST TO HELP:

- Remember, **healing is an inside job.**

- **Awareness** is always the first step to transforming anything. Once you're aware of your problem, you can research new solutions, experiment to see what works for you, and own your healing.

- Always **advocate for your own healing.** No one else is responsible for your health. Own it and advocate for exactly what you need.

- **Set goals for continuous growth and improvement.** Consider finding a mentor, coach, or accountability partner to stay on track.

- **Set anchors** as friendly reminders to make progress towards your goals. Download a copy of the Anchors Worksheet at https://coachhollyjackson.activehosted.com/f/52

- If you aren't growing and learning, you're moving backward.

I encourage you to set anchors. Use the tools throughout this book. Print things that will help you stay on track. Set goals and share them to help you stay on track.

Celebrate your progress, even the small stuff.

Remember, healing is a journey. It lasts a lifetime. Try to enjoy every step, every season, every summit, and even every setback.

Remember, it takes baby steps. One step every day will get you 1% closer to your goal. What action can you take to grow, get healthier, and feel better?

You've got this!

12

THRIVE!

*"There's only one corner of the universe
you can be certain of improving
and that's your own self."*

~ALDOUS HUXLEY

I used to think that there were limits on what I could do in life. I believed the doctors when they told me I would never live a full life, I couldn't go skydiving, I shouldn't have a child naturally, or I should go on disability.

But when my friend had the courage to tell me that I had somehow lost myself, it sent a jolt through me. It woke me up! I'm forever grateful to my good friend, Martina—for loving me enough to tell me. For having the courage to say something. To take a bold stance.

From that moment on, I have been on a journey. A journey to heal myself. A journey to up-level my beliefs and identity. A journey to share what I have learned with the world.

I don't want you to suffer for years like I did. Those years are forever lost. I missed out on moments, memories, and opportunities. I lost myself and allowed others to define success for me. And I was deeply unhappy because of that. I was living a life of victimhood. I wasn't choosing to live my life fully. I was living a muted half-life for far too long.

But here's the good news. You don't have to hit rock bottom. You don't have to struggle and suffer for years like I did. You can take this book and use it as a blueprint—a roadmap to healing—a toolbox to transform. I beg you, start today. Take one small step *today*. Do *not* wait. If you do, days will go by. Months will pass by. Years will blur by you. And You'll miss out. You'll suffer. You'll struggle. You'll experience pain beyond what you think is possible.

Take action today because you're worth it. You have loved ones around you rooting for you; you have family cheering you from the sidelines, waiting for you to wake up and take your life back. If you take nothing else from this book, I hope you take action. Action that helps you grow. Action that allows you to heal. Action that gets you out of the victim mindset and into an empowered state of being. Action that allows you to grow and thrive.

All it takes is one small step every day. With each small baby step, you grow one percent. If you do that every single day, you'll have grown three hundred and sixty-five percent every single year.

But if you don't take action, you'll slide backward. And when you slide backward, the slide can be exponential. It steals your joy. It steals your presence. It steals your identity.

Don't let fear hold you back. Take action today!

THE JOURNEY

Friend, we have been on quite a journey together. The campfire has had its moments of intensity, its moments of sadness, its moments of familiarity, and many moments of connection.

We have talked about inspiration and how it's the foundation of transformation, how it helps us breathe in new ideas, fresh perspectives, and the energy required to grow.

As you continue your health journey, I want you to remember to tap into what inspires you. It's your life force. It's your encouragement. Your empowerment. Your strength when you feel weak. Your power when you feel disempowered and discouraged. Your foundation when you feel your life is upside down. Your stability when you feel terrified at what life has thrown at you.

Dig deep.

ALWAYS COME BACK TO INSPIRATION AND GRATITUDE

List out every single thing you're grateful for. Celebrate your wins—even the small ones. Remember, change is inevitable. Life is constantly throwing us curve balls. Nothing is set in stone . . . ever. To thrive, you must remain flexible. In flow. Ready to continually grow. Prepared to face anything and everything along this crazy adventure we call life.

And now, you're equipped to handle it all. Anything life throws at you. Your health is your wealth. You know how to continuously improve your health. Your energy. Your self-care. Your self-talk and confidence. Your relationship with food and what you eat. Your sleep and how to best energize your body.

You know how to reduce and manage your stress and anxiety. You understand the importance of your health. You understand that you're not a victim. That you own your healing journey. That you're responsible for your health and your life. That you can do anything you set your mind to because you *are* powerful.

STEP INTO YOUR POWER

You're strong. You're powerful. Miracles are possible. Own your journey today and thrive. The only possible outcome when you own your healing journey is to thrive! When you refuse to be a victim. When you refuse to take no for an answer. When you refuse to accept something that you've heard from a doctor that limits you. When you choose to believe something that's more inspired. More empowered. More exciting. More healing.

WHEN YOU STEP INTO YOUR PERSONAL POWER, YOU BREAK FREE FROM CHAINS

You pave the way for others following in your wake. You become a leader to others in chronic pain. You become a light in the world when others only see darkness.

When we choose to heal ourselves, we are doing some of the most important work in this world. Because when we transform our lives, it shows others what's possible. I want to help millions wake up from victimhood. To stop letting others define what they believe about themselves and about life. To stop isolation, loneliness, and depression.

When we choose inspiration, and we step into our own personal power, anything is possible. There are no limits. There is only possibility.

Stepping into your personal power is a choice you make over and over again.

Every single morning when I wake up, I get to consciously choose. Do I choose a day of power and inspiration? Or do I choose a day of victimhood and isolation?

It's a choice. And only *you* have the power to make it. With every moment, I urge you to ask yourself, "What do I choose at this moment? What choice would make me feel better, more excited, inspired, and joyful?" Pause to tune into your body and listen. Choose whatever brings you inspiration, joy, love, and openness. Say no to anything that brings you tension, anxiety, stress, or pain.

Choosing personal power takes practice. You may find yourself facing a new health challenge or pain. That can be triggering. It can bring back old habits. Old beliefs. That's okay. The important thing is to recognize it and stop the old pattern by choosing something new.

When you feel yourself spiraling into anxiety, stress, overwhelm, or anger, hit pause. Get curious. Where is this coming from? Ask yourself, "Am I choosing inspiration, or did I fall back into victimhood?" If you fell back into victimhood, be grateful that you were able to recognize the pattern and choose again. Choose inspiration. Choose ownership of your journey.

Anything is possible when we choose again. When we break old habits and patterns. When we choose inspiration and healing, there are no limits.

PAUSE AND REFLECT

I want you to take a moment. Pause and reflect on everything you have learned. Everything you have changed. How much better you feel today compared to when you started reading this book.

In chapter one, you learned about inspiration and why it's so important. In chapter two, you learned how to apply that inspiration to your life in tangible ways.

NEVER FORGET TO TAP BACK INTO WHAT INSPIRES YOU

Use that inspiration to take action. To push through fear. To get through the pain. To bust through walls. In chapter three, you discovered that your health is your wealth. That without health, you have nothing. Your body is your vessel in this lifetime.

WHAT WE DO WITH OUR HEALTH EITHER HOLDS US BACK OR ALLOWS US TO SOAR TO NEW HEIGHTS

Are you choosing to amplify your health? To continuously grow and improve? What goals have you set for your health journey? I hope you have set *big* goals. The more you stretch yourself to grow in your health, the more capacity you have to face anything in life.

In chapter four, you discovered how important sleep is to your healing process. It's important to your mental and emotional health. It allows you to heal through rest and restoration. When faced with new challenges in life, never sacrifice your sleep.

SLEEP AND REST ARE THE ROOT OF HEALING

If you only change one thing in your health journey, work on your sleep. It's the biggest needle-mover in healing.

In chapter five, you learned about the importance of self-care. You discovered that It's not selfish.

WHEN WE TAKE CARE OF OURSELVES, IT ALLOWS US TO GIVE MORE. TO BE MORE PRESENT

We show up as the best version of ourselves when we invest in our self-care. During my meditation this morning, I read a short excerpt about a woman who had an epiphany. She wasn't allowing space for creativity. She decided to prioritize creativity. For her, that meant painting and art.

Every morning, she chose to spend time painting and working with her art instead of starting with chores. After doing that for a week, she discovered that she had more energy to do her chores. And she showed up happy and more joyful with her family. Everyone loved the shift. And everything still got done.

What are you lacking in your life that would bring you more energy? What if you prioritized that? What would that open up for you?

NEVER STOP EXPERIMENTING

Transformation requires us to be curious scientists, always willing to learn and try new things, even when they're uncomfortable.

In chapter six, you learned that stress and anxiety kill. It depletes us— brings pain and tension to our bodies.

STRESS AND ANXIETY ARE WITHIN OUR POWER TO MANAGE AND REDUCE

You found new tools and strategies to reduce your stress and anxiety. Stress and anxiety are always there. It's how we choose to interact with them that matters. I hope you're using those tools and finding new ones that work for you.

In chapter seven, you explored your self-talk and how important your mental health is. How we speak to ourselves influences how we see the world, how we feel, how and if we take action. Uncovering your negative and limiting beliefs and working to shift them is the foundation to transformation.

You learned techniques and tools to uncover and shift your limiting thoughts and beliefs. That work takes time and is ongoing. It never stops. There is always something new you can transform because there are no limits.

I hope you continue to grow and release old thoughts and beliefs limiting your health, life, and power.

MOVEMENTENT IS PART OF THE HEALING EXPERIENCE—IT HELPS THE BODY HEAL AND IS PART OF THE HUMAN EXPERIENCE

Movement is at the root of taking action. Therefore, movement is essential for thriving success.

In chapter eight we explored the importance of movement and how to build your personal movement menu. We even explored five strategies to break through any resistance you might be feeling around movement.

I hope you took action on this and are finding yourself falling in love with movement. I hope you have found joy and creativity during the process of exploration.

As you release the old, it allows you to step into even bigger goals and visions for your life.

In chapter nine, we looked at food and the importance of what we eat, and how we are when we eat. We got curious and did some experiments around what best fuels our bodies. You got new tools to help you eat without stress.

YOUR RELATIONSHIP WITH FOOD IS VERY TELLING—IT TELLS YOU WHEN YOU'RE TRYING TO NUMB OUT LIFE

It tells you when you're in a healthy phase. It tells you when you're being obsessive. Pay attention to your relationship with food, then shift to something that fuels you and brings you the most energy.

In chapter ten, we explored chronic pain. You got a framework to help heal it—to transform your relationship with pain—to be the advocate for your health and healing.

NOT ALLOWING CHRONIC PAIN TO BE YOUR IDENTITY IS A CHOICE—REFUSING TO BE THE VICTIM IS THE HARDEST BUT MOST EMPOWERING CHOICE YOU'LL EVER MAKE

It takes time, but if you use the framework and tools within this chapter, you'll be able to live with your pain. Instead of it ruling your life, you'll know how to work with your pain. You can do anything, even if you have chronic pain. It does not define who you are. It does not define your life. It cannot place limitations on you unless you allow it to.

In chapter eleven, you were sworn in to own your health journey.

YOU KNOW THE SECRET TO HEALING—IT'S AN INSIDE JOB AND ONLY YOU CAN HEAL AND TRANSFORM YOURSELF

No one else can do the work for you. No one else can wave a magic wand and fix you or your world. Only you have that power. And thank goodness. Because you're creating the best life for you. Only you know what will bring you the most joy, inspiration, excitement, energy, and love!

You deserve a life of health. You deserve a life full of inspiration. You deserve a life of constant growth and endless possibilities. You deserve to live the life of your dreams.

It's time for you to turn your light on full force. It's time for you to own your health. It's time for you to live your life full out.

It's time for YOU to thrive!

GET THE HEALTH SECRETS
TO RAVING SUCCESS MASTER CLASS

You are in the right place if you are tired of feeling exhausted, depleted, burnt out, sick, and in pain. You are in the right place if you are healthy but want even more energy and vitality.

In this five-day course, we dive into the concepts in this book (and more) to amplify your health—to build a strong foundation of health, rest, self-care, and energy.

The course provides videos, audio recordings, worksheets, and tools that you can start putting into action today. If you are tired of reading a book but not taking action, this is your solution.

Learn the tools, tactics, and methods to change your habits. Build new behaviors that give you more health. And much more!

SIGN UP TODAY IF YOU ARE:

- Ready to get more and better sleep
- Committed to becoming pain-free
- Excited to fix your self-talk
- Ready to reduce your stress and anxiety
- Committed to owning your health journey
- Excited to thrive!

LEARN MORE ABOUT THE CLASS AND SIGN UP TODAY:

https://hollyjeanjackson.com/healthsecrets

Remember, healing begins as soon as you choose to take action. So, choose again and take action today that matches the size of your dreams.

Take action that gets you one percent closer to a healthy and thriving you.

With one percent of growth every day, we open the door to growing three hundred and sixty-five percent within the year.

You deserve a life of health.

You deserve a life of vitality.

You deserve a life of success.

You deserve the life of your dreams. Take action today. You've got this!

———————

MEET AND HIRE YOUR HOLISTIC BUSINESS COACH

Through Holistic Business Coaching, Holly helps mission-driven entrepreneurs and business owners start, build, or scale their businesses without burning out. She specializes in working with health and wellness businesses.

Holly's clients learn how to cope with stress, define their life priorities, and rediscover their passion for business. She helps them see their blind spots that often cost them exposure, clients, and income.

For over twelve years, Holly has provided insights, strategies, and fresh perspectives.

Holly says, "My clients can expect accountability, growth, and a step-by-step game plan for success. I believe every professional must develop their internal compass and decide what their legacy will be. Holistic coaching goes beyond helping your business and helps the whole person."

If you are an entrepreneur or business owner and want to contact Holly, please . . .

SCHEDULE YOUR DISCOVERY COACHING CALL AT

https://hollyjeanjackson.com/services/schedule-appointment/

Email her with your questions at holly@hollyjeanjackson.com

HIRE HOLLY TO SPEAK AT YOUR COMPANY OR EVENT

Holly Jean Jackson helps entrepreneurs and business leaders love their life and business again. With over twelve years of technology and business experience, she helps business leaders get their groove back physically, mentally, and emotionally.

She does this through a combined approach of both coaching and consulting, providing practical and actionable results. She also helps end fear and frustration with technology.

Holly teaches her clients to remember self-care is essential, not optional. And that community is critical to success. Many entrepreneurs and business owners are crumbling under the pressure to perform, and they're worried that burnout will ultimately crush their dreams. The busyness of life can take you off track and keep you at bay. Success can be mastered. Using my three-step proprietary process, entrepreneurs can up-level their confidence, passion and finally succeed.

Holly's signature talk is called *From Failure to Prosperity*. She also has a business essentials series which can be offered as a workshop, breakout session, or keynote. The Business Essential Series covers The Power of Video, Build Your Brand Through Story, and 3 Business Time Savers (3 core business technologies every biz owner needs). She also offers a workshop called Visualize Your Year and Make it Happen, usually offered at the beginning of the New Year.

To learn more about her speaking topics, portfolio, and testimonials, visit her speaking page at https://hollyjeanjackson.com/speaking/

DOWNLOAD A COPY OF HOLLY'S SPEAKER KIT AT
https://hollyjeanjackson.com/speaking/

BOOK YOUR SPEAKING CONSULTATION CALL AT
https://businessnetworkchat.as.me/schedule.php?appointmentType=11798478

JOIN THE
BUSINESS BUILDER THROWDOWN
NINJA MASTERMIND COMMUNITY

Are you tired of building your biz *alone*?

Are you burnt out on trying to have all the answers without a community of fellow biz ninjas?

We know the world is feeling the burden of *isolation*. Humans are built for connection. Between this pandemic and its financial impacts on biz owners, we know you have been hit even harder.

It's difficult enough to navigate this new world as a human. It's even more challenging as a business owner and entrepreneur. We are looking for biz ninjas, just like *you*.

WHAT'S IN IT FOR YOU:

- Mastermind Community
- Weekly Office Hours *live* Meeting with Business Growth Experts
- Access to courses like Inbox Mastery and Podcast Mastery
- Peer Support - People to Talk To Who Understand Your Struggles
- Referral Opportunities

Isolation isn't just depressing, it's bad for you, and it's bad for your business.

It's time to join a business-minded community that understands what you're going through and can support you and your goals.

Experts, office hours, peer support, courses, challenges, networking...to improve your BUSINESS and your LIFE.

THE ENEMIES OF YOUR BUSINESS ARE OUT THERE!

They are obscurity, isolation, overwhelm, information overload, lack of focus, and having more problems than time to solve them. Business Builder Ninjas is a dedicated mastermind community that solves all of these problems.

BECOME A BIZ NINJA TODAY AT

https://www.businessbuilderthrowdown.com/ninjas

ACKNOWLEDGMENTS

I could not have done this without the support of my family. To my mother for pouring wisdom, love, and creativity into my life. For always listening and supporting no matter how dark things appeared. For taking the time to show me the beauty of this world. For instilling in me so much creativity and spark and gusto for life that it pours over and into this book. You are my inspiration. You have one of the purest souls I have ever come across in this lifetime. Your love, generosity, playfulness, and focus on fun in this life are contagious. I am proud to call you my mother and friend, Heather Surratt.

To my partner and twin flame, Ian Baens, for seeing me for me. For being willing to call me on my stuff and still love me for who I am. For challenging me to be more vulnerable and honest in my relationships. For being a mirror to my soul in a safe space that allows me to heal my own baggage. For never judging me but choosing to love and accept me instead. For always encouraging me to write, even on those days when I felt resistance. For supporting me and showing me how proud you are. You are my constant shining star—my compass to this beautiful life we are continuing to build—my light in the darkness.

To my sister, Melissa Ragan, for always making me laugh even on days where I felt depressed or like nothing would ever work in my business. You bring me so much hope for my future family. You are the most amazing mom and wise beyond your years. Thanks for being my rock when things feel like they are crumbling.

To my brother, Tim Jackson, for your commitment and dedication to serving our country in the marine corp and on our home lines as a nurse during the pandemic. You are an amazing example of living your passion. Thank you for being true to your calling. You are an amazing father and husband to your family. Thanks for bringing more health and joy to the world.

To my stepdad, Phil Surratt, for always being a support system to my entire family. You have the kindest heart and soul. Thanks for always lending an ear to listen and for offering hugs in hard times. Thank you for always being there for our crazy family. I look forward to our future adventures including our bucket list goal of hiking part of the Appalachian trail together.

To my publisher, Laura Di Franco, thank you for helping me get unstuck and finally write the first of three books. Without you, none of this would be possible. You helped me see that all my excuses were just that . . . excuses. Thanks for helping me get past my own BS and into action. This was one of the most healing processes I have ever experienced. And it never would have started without you.

To my best friend and sister for life, Martina Martinez. You are my heart and soul. You always remind me of just how badass we really are. You help me see my progress even when it seems small. You call me on my stuff because you love me. Without you, I would have lost myself many years ago. Thank you for having the courage and fierce love for our friendship to be honest with me. Your vulnerability and strength constantly amaze me. I hope my future daughter has that same fierceness within her.

To my business coach, Hope Zvara. Thank you for being my constant cheerleader and constant butt-kicker. Without you, I wouldn't be where I am today. You breathe fresh ideas, perspectives, and new ideas into my life and business. Thank you for reminding me that I can have it all: a kickass business and a family. I can be blissfully happy, and that's the key to success. I am so grateful our paths crossed.

To my life coach, Sara Paine. Thank you for your continued spiritual support and prayers. Without your continued wisdom pouring into my life, I am certain I would have given up years ago. You reminded me along the way of all the progress I was making. You showed me that success isn't always linear. It has its ups and downs, and when we plant seeds and keep our faith and hope, success can be exponential. And guess what?! Those seeds I planted are finally taking off to exponential degrees! Thank you for your wisdom and heart, my dear friend.

To my energy healer and coach, Will Smith. Thank you for your constant support. I am a very sensitive soul, and without you, I would be lost. You have given me new avenues for healing. New tools for navigating life. Without you, I would still be facing the world as "boss babe" and leaving out intimacy, creativity, and harmony. You are an amazing and talented healer in this world, and I am so grateful I am part of your journey of bringing your talents to the world.

To my dear friend, Veronica Silva. Thank you for your constant encouragement and friendship. You have always reminded me that I have a gift. That I have something special to share with the world. You remind me every day of the value of community, love, support, spiritual growth, and presence. You are one of my soul sisters for life. I am forever grateful that we are friends and kindred spirits for life. That we get to do life together.

To my friend and website manager, Dean Jensen. Thank you for standing by me, mentoring me in my early days, and encouraging me even in my darkest moments. For helping me make my website beautiful and, in particular, making the Health Secrets for Raving Success Class a success. Without you, none of this would be possible. I am grateful to have you in my life as a friend, sounding board, creator, and web guru.

To my father, Elvis Jackson. Thank you for showing me what hard work looks like. For showing me the entrepreneurial spirit at a young age. For walking the talk of loyalty, family, sacrifice, and constant growth. I am honored that I get to build my business on the same foundations that you taught me at a young age. I wish you were here to celebrate this milestone with me. My heart is with you wherever you are. I love you to the moon and back.

To my friends, family, and community. Thank you for sharing your life with me. For being willing to be vulnerable. For sharing yourself authentically. For accepting me for me—emotional, intense, strong-headed, stubborn, and powerful. Thanks for making space for me in your life.

This life is pointless unless we remove our masks. We must be courageous and faithful. We must bear our souls and be authentic if we ever want to live more fully. If we ever want to heal ourselves and the world around us, we must be the change we want to see.

ABOUT THE AUTHOR

HOLLY JEAN JACKSON

Holly Jean Jackson grew up outside of Chicago, Illinois, and then moved to Winston-Salem, North Carolina, with her family and grandparents. She started falling in love with writing at a very young age and even won a poetry contest in middle school.

She attended Elmhurst College for undergraduate school and was awarded a double major in Political Science and Urban Studies with a minor in music performance. She loves music and playing piano and clarinet but didn't want to lose her joy for it. After taking a year off, she attended graduate school at North Carolina State University, studying Public Administration with a minor in Non-Profits.

In 2004, she began her career in nonprofit and public sector education. After moving to California, she eventually took a corporate job at Visa (the credit card company). She held various technology leadership roles at many large companies for several years.

After facing layoff after layoff, coupled with new health struggles, she found herself re-evaluating life. She decided to build her own business, paving the way for others to do the same through her coaching.

She now works with business owners and entrepreneurs who want to start and scale the business of their dreams. She helps her clients define and build the legacy they wish to leave behind. Her company, Holly Jean Jackson LLC, provides holistic business coaching, marketing consulting, speaking, and mastermind services for hundreds of clients all around the world.

Holly's long-term vision is to build a nonprofit for children working with school systems around the country, focusing on self-help, soft skills, and entrepreneurship. She wants to empower children and communities to think about education pathways in a different way. She believes that every child deserves access to skills and tools that our school systems simply can't provide, like budgeting, meditation, yoga, financial planning, and entrepreneurship.

Holly currently resides in Raleigh, North Carolina, with her partner, Ian Baens. In her free time, she enjoys traveling the world, reading, writing, cycling, hiking, swimming, playing the piano, and spending time with family and friends.

*"The place of true healing is a fierce place.
It's a giant place.
It's a place of monstrous beauty
and endless dark and glimmering light.
And you have to work really, really,
really hard to get there,
but you can do it."*

~ CHERYL STRAYED